AAT

Q2022

Personal Tax
Finance Act 2021

EXAM KIT

This Exam Kit supports study for the following AAT qualifications:

AAT Level 4 Diploma in Professional Accounting

AAT Diploma in Professional Accounting at SCQF Level 8

KAPLAN

PUBLISHING

British Library Cataloguing-in-Publication Data

A catalogue record for this book is available from the British Library.

Published by:

Kaplan Publishing UK

Unit 2 The Business Centre

Molly Millar's Lane

Wokingham

Berkshire

RG41 2QZ

ISBN: 978-1-83996-067-3

© Kaplan Financial Limited, 2021

Printed and bound in Great Britain

Acknowledgements

We are grateful to HM Revenue and Customs for the provision of tax forms, which are Crown Copyright and are reproduced here with kind permission from the Office of Public Sector Information.

Kaplan Publishing are constantly finding new ways to support students looking for exam success and our online resources really do add an extra dimension to your studies.

This book comes with free MyKaplan online resources so that you can study anytime, anywhere. **This free online resource is not sold separately and is included in the price of the book.**

Having purchased this book, you have access to the following online study materials:

CONTENT	AAT	
	Text	Kit
Electronic version of the book	✓	✓
Knowledge Check tests with instant answers	✓	
Mock assessments online	✓	✓
Material updates	✓	✓

How to access your online resources

Received this book as part of your Kaplan course?
If you have a MyKaplan account, your full online resources will be added automatically, in line with the information in your course confirmation email. If you've not used MyKaplan before, you'll be sent an activation email once your resources are ready.

Bought your book from Kaplan?
We'll automatically add your online resources to your MyKaplan account. If you've not used MyKaplan before, you'll be sent an activation email.

Bought your book from elsewhere?
Go to **www.mykaplan.co.uk/add-online-resources**
Enter the ISBN number found on the title page and back cover of this book.
Add the unique pass key number contained in the scratch panel below.
You may be required to enter additional information during this process to set up or confirm your account details.

This code can only be used once for the registration of this book online. This registration and your online content will expire when the examinations covered by this book have taken place. Please allow one hour from the time you submit your book details for us to process your request.

Please scratch the film to access your unique code.

Please be aware that this code is case-sensitive and you will need to include the dashes within the passcode, but not when entering the ISBN.

PUBLISHING

CONTENTS

Features in this exam kit

In addition to providing a wide ranging bank of real assessment style questions, we have also included in this kit:

- unit specific information and advice on assessment technique
- our recommended approach to make your revision for this particular unit as effective as possible.

You will find a wealth of other resources to help you with your studies on the Kaplan and AAT websites:

www.mykaplan.co.uk

www.aat.org.uk/

Quality and accuracy are of the utmost importance to us so if you spot an error in any of our products, please send an email to mykaplanreporting@kaplan.com with full details, or follow the link to the feedback form in MyKaplan.

Our Quality Coordinator will work with our technical team to verify the error and take action to ensure it is corrected in future editions.

UNIT SPECIFIC INFORMATION

THE ASSESSMENT

FORMAT OF THE ASSESSMENT

Learners will be assessed by computer-based assessment.

In any one assessment, learners may not be assessed on all content, or on the full depth or breadth of a piece of content. The content assessed may change over time to ensure validity of assessment, but all assessment criteria will be tested over time.

The learning outcomes for this unit are as follows:

	Learning outcome	Weighting
1	Understand principles and rules that underpin taxation systems	10%
2	Calculate a UK taxpayer's total income	20%
3	Calculate income tax and National Insurance contributions (NICs) payable by UK taxpayers	30%
4	Calculate capital gains tax payable by UK taxpayers	30%
5	Understand the principles of inheritance tax	10%
	Total	100%

Time allowed

2 hours

PASS MARK

The pass mark for all AAT CBAs is 70%.

 Always keep your eye on the clock and make sure you attempt all questions!

DETAILED SYLLABUS

The detailed syllabus and study guide written by the AAT can be found at:

www.aat.org.uk

INDEX TO QUESTIONS AND ANSWERS

ANSWER ENHANCEMENTS

We have added the following enhancements to the answers in this exam kit:

Key answer tips

Some answers include key answer tips to help your understanding of each question.

Tutorial note

Some answers include tutorial notes to explain some of the technical points in more detail.

ASSESSMENT TECHNIQUE

- **Do not skip any of the** material in the syllabus.

- **Read each question** *very* carefully.

- In calculative style questions if you are provided with rounding rules (e.g. round to the nearest pence) you **must** follow these to gain credit.

- **Double-check your answer** before committing yourself to it.

- Answer **every** question – if you do not know an answer to a multiple choice question or true/false question, you don't lose anything by guessing. Think carefully before you **guess**.

- If you are answering a multiple-choice question, **eliminate first those answers that you know are wrong**. Then choose the most appropriate answer from those that are left.

- **Don't panic** if you realise you've answered a question incorrectly. Getting one question wrong will not mean the difference between passing and failing.

COMPUTER-BASED ASSESSMENTS – TIPS

- Do not attempt a CBA until you have **completed all study material** relating to it.

- On the AAT website there is a CBA demonstration. It is **ESSENTIAL** that you attempt this before your real CBA. You will become familiar with how to move around the CBA screens and the way that questions are formatted, increasing your confidence and speed in the actual assessment.

- Be sure you understand how to use the **software** before you start the assessment. If in doubt, ask the assessment centre staff to explain it to you.

- Questions are **displayed on the screen** and answers are entered using keyboard and mouse. At the end of the assessment, you are given a certificate showing the result you have achieved unless some manual marking is required for the assessment.

- In addition to the traditional multiple-choice question type, CBAs will also contain **other types of questions**, such as number entry questions, drag and drop, true/false, pick lists or drop down menus or hybrids of these.

- In some CBAs you may have to type in complete computations or written answers.

- You need to be sure you **know how to answer questions** of this type before you sit the real assessment, through practice.

KAPLAN'S RECOMMENDED REVISION APPROACH

QUESTION PRACTICE IS THE KEY TO SUCCESS

Success in professional examinations relies upon you acquiring a firm grasp of the required knowledge at the tuition phase. In order to be able to do the questions, knowledge is essential.

However, the difference between success and failure often hinges on your assessment technique on the day and making the most of the revision phase of your studies.

The **Kaplan study text** is the starting point, designed to provide the underpinning knowledge to tackle all questions. However, in the revision phase, poring over textbooks is not the answer.

Kaplan pocket notes are designed to help you quickly revise a topic area; however, you then need to practise questions. There is a need to progress to assessment style questions as soon as possible, and to tie your assessment technique and technical knowledge together.

The importance of question practice cannot be over-emphasised.

The recommended approach below is designed by expert tutors in the field, in conjunction with their knowledge of the chief assessor and the sample assessment.

You need to practise as many questions as possible in the time you have left.

OUR AIM

Our aim is to get you to the stage where you can attempt assessment questions confidently, to time, in a closed book environment, with no supplementary help (i.e. to simulate the real assessment experience).

Practising your assessment technique is also vitally important for you to assess your progress and identify areas of weakness that may need more attention in the final run up to the real assessment.

In order to achieve this we recognise that initially you may feel the need to practise some questions with open book help.

Good assessment technique is vital.

THE KAPLAN REVISION PLAN

STAGE 1: ASSESS AREAS OF STRENGTH AND WEAKNESS

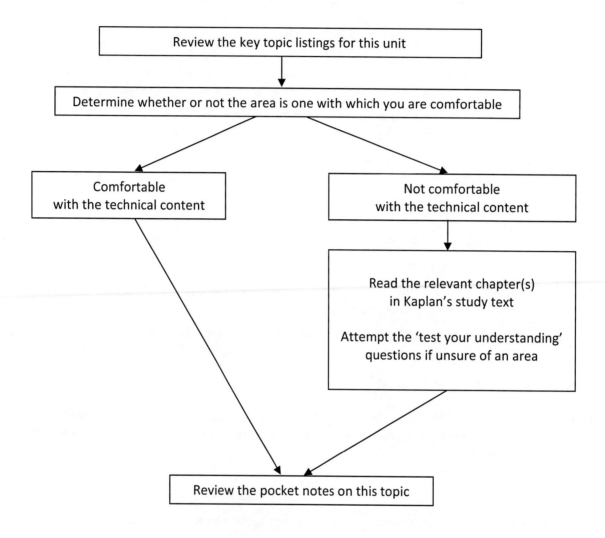

STAGE 2: PRACTICE QUESTIONS

Follow the order of revision of topics as presented in this kit and attempt the questions in the order suggested.

Try to avoid referring to study texts and your notes and the model answer until you have completed your attempt.

Review your attempt with the model answer and assess how much of the answer you achieved.

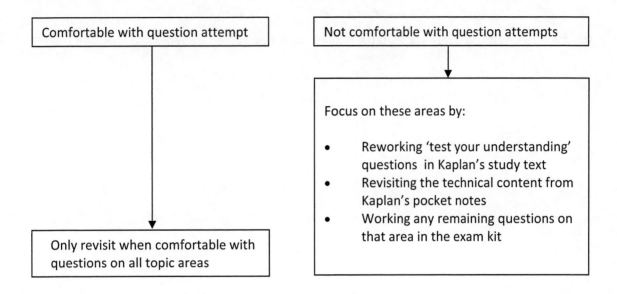

STAGE 3: FINAL PRE-REAL ASSESSMENT REVISION

We recommend that you **attempt at least one full mock assessment** containing a set of previously unseen real assessment standard questions.

Attempt the mock CBA online in timed, closed book conditions to simulate the real assessment experience.

You will find a mock CBA for this unit at www.mykaplan.co.uk

REFERENCE INFORMATION

Reference material is provided in this assessment. During your assessment you will be able to access reference material through a series of clickable links on the right of every task. These will produce pop-up windows which can be moved or closed.

The reference material has been included in this exam kit (below). This is based on the version of the reference material that was available at the time of going to print.

The full version of the reference material is available for download from the AAT website.

KAPLAN PUBLISHING

Level 4 Personal Tax (PNTA)
reference material

Finance Act 2021 – for Q2022 assessments in 2022 and 2023

Introduction

This document comprises data that you may need to consult during your Personal Tax computer-based assessment.

The material can be consulted during the practice and live assessments by using the reference materials section at each task position. It's made available here so you can familiarise yourself with the content before the assessment.

Do not take a print of this document into the exam room with you*.

This document may be changed to reflect periodical updates in the computer-based assessment, so please check you have the most recent version while studying. This version is based on **Finance Act 2021** and is for use in AAT Q2022 assessments in 2022 and 2023.

*Unless you need a printed version as part of reasonable adjustments for particular needs, in which case you must discuss this with your tutor at least six weeks before the assessment date.

Contents

1. Tax rates and bands

Tax rates	Tax bands	Normal rates %	Dividend rates %
Basic rate	£ 1–£37,700	20	7.5
Higher rate	£37,701–£150,000	40	32.5
Additional rate	£150,001 and over	45	38.1

2. Allowances

		£
Personal allowance		12,570
Savings allowance:	Basic rate taxpayer	1,000
	Higher rate taxpayer	500
Dividend allowance		2,000
Income limit for personal allowances*		100,000

* Personal allowances are reduced by £1 for every £2 over the income limit.

3. Property income allowance

	£
Annual limit	1,000

4. Individual savings accounts

	£
Annual limit	20,000

5. Deemed domicile

Deemed domicile	Criteria
Condition A	Was born in the UK
	Domicile of origin was in the UK
	Was resident in the UK for 2017 to 2018 or later years
Condition B	Has been UK resident for at least 15 of the 20 tax years immediately before the relevant tax year

6. Residence

Residence	Criteria
Automatically resident	Spend 183 or more days in the UK in the tax year; or
	Only home is in the UK; and
	You owned, rented or lived in the home for at least 91 days and spent at least 30 days there in the tax year.
Automatically not resident	Spend fewer than 16 days in the UK (or 46 days if you have not been classed as UK resident for the three previous tax years; or
	Work abroad full time (averaging at least 35 hours a week) and spend less than 91 days in the UK, of which no more than 30 are spent working
Resident by number of ties	If UK resident for one or more of the previous three tax years: • 4 ties needed if spend 16-45 days in the UK • 3 ties needed if spend 46-90 days in the UK • 2 ties needed if spend 91-120 days in the UK • 1 tie needed if spend over 120 days in the UK.
	If UK resident in none of the previous three tax years: • 4 ties needed if spend 46-90 days in the UK • 3 ties needed if spend 91-120 days in the UK • 2 ties needed if spend over 120 days in the UK.

7. Car benefit percentage

CO$_2$ Emissions for petrol engines g/km	Electric range miles	Cars first registered from 6 April 2020 %
Nil		1
1 to 50	130 or more	1
1 to 50	70-129	4
1 to 50	40-69	7
1 to 50	30-39	11
1 to 50	Less than 30	13
51 to 54		14
55 or more		15 + 1% for every extra 5g/km above 55g/km
Registration pre 6 April 2020*		Additional 1%
Diesel engines**		Additional 4%

* The additional 1% is not applied where the CO$_2$ emissions are Nil.

**The additional 4% will not apply to diesel cars which are registered after 1 September 2017 and meet the RDE2 standards.

8. Car fuel benefit

	£
Base figure	24,600

9. Approved mileage allowance payments (employees and residential landlords)

First 10,000 miles	45p per mile
Over 10,000 miles	25p per mile
Additional passengers	5p per mile per passenger
Motorcycles	24p per mile
Bicycles	20p per mile

10. Van benefit charge

	£
Basic charge	3,500
Private fuel charge	669
Benefit charge for zero emission vans	NIL

11. Other benefits in kind

Benefit	Notes
Expensive accommodation limit	£75,000
Health screening	One per year
Incidental overnight expenses: within UK	£5 per night
Incidental overnight expenses: overseas	£10 per night
Job-related accommodation	£Nil
Living expenses where job-related exemption applies	Restricted to 10% of employees net earnings
Loan of assets annual charge	20%
Low-rate or interest free loans	Up to £10,000
Mobile telephones	One per employee
Non-cash gifts from someone other than the employer	£250 per tax year
Non-cash long service award	£50 per year of service
Pay whilst attending a full-time course	£15,480 per academic year
Provision of eye tests and spectacles for VDU use	£Nil
Provision of parking spaces	£Nil
Provision of workplace childcare	£Nil
Provision of workplace sports facilities	£Nil
Removal and relocation expenses	£8,000
Staff party or event	£150 per head
Staff suggestion scheme	Up to £5,000
Subsidised meals	£Nil
Working from home	£6 per week/£26 per month

12. HMRC official rate

	%
HMRC official rate	**2**

13. National insurance contributions

		%
Class 1 Employee:	Below £9,568	0
	Above £9,568 and Below £50,270	12
	£50,270 and above	2
Class 1 Employer:	Below £8,840	0
	£8,840 and above	13.8
Class 1A		13.8
		£
Employment allowance		4,000

14. Capital gains tax

	£
Annual exempt amount	12,300

15. Capital gains tax – tax rates

	%
Basic rate	10
Higher rate	20

16. Inheritance tax – tax rates

		£
Nil rate band		325,000
Additional residence nil-rate band*		175,000

		%
Excess taxable at:	Death rate	40
	Lifetime rate	20

* Applies when a home is passed on death to direct descendants of the deceased after 6 April 2017. Any unused band is transferrable to a spouse or civil partner.

17. Inheritance tax – tapering relief

	% reduction
3 years or less	0
Over 3 years but less than 4 years	20
Over 4 years but less than 5 years	40
Over 5 years but less than 6 years	60
Over 6 years but less than 7 years	80

18. Inheritance tax – exemptions

		£
Small gifts		250 per transferee per tax year
Marriage or civil partnership:	From parent	5,000
	Grandparent	2,500
	One party to the other	2,500
	Others	1,000
Annual exemption		3,000

The Association of Accounting Technicians
140 Aldersgate Street
London
EC1A 4HY
t: +44 (0)20 7397 3000
f: +44 (0)20 7397 3009
e: aat@aat.org.uk
aat.org.uk

Level 4 Personal Tax (PNTA)
reference material

Professional conduct in relation to taxation

Finance Act 2021 – for Q2022 assessments in 2022 and 2023

Reference material for AAT assessment of Personal Tax

Introduction

This document comprises data that you may need to consult during your Personal Tax computer-based assessment. The material can be consulted during the practice and live assessments by using the reference material section at each task position. It is made available here so you can familiarise yourself with the content before the assessment.

Do not take a print of this document into the exam room with you*.

This document may be changed to reflect periodical updates in the computer-based assessment, so please check you have the most recent version while studying. This version is based on **Finance Act 2021** and is for use in AAT assessments in 2022 and 2023.

* Unless you need a printed version as part of reasonable adjustments for particular needs, in which case you must discuss this with your tutor at least six weeks before the assessment date.

Contents

1. Interpretation and abbreviations

Context

Tax advisors operate in a complex business and financial environment. The increasing public focus on the role of taxation in wider society means a greater interest in the actions of tax advisors and their clients.

This guidance, written by the professional bodies for their members working in tax, sets out the hallmarks of a good tax advisor, and in particular the fundamental principles of behaviour that members are expected to follow.

Interpretation

1.1   In this guidance:
- 'Client' includes, where the context requires, 'former client'
- 'Member' (and 'members') includes 'firm' or 'practice' and the staff thereof
- Words in the singular include the plural and words in the plural include the singular.

Abbreviations

1.2   The following abbreviations have been used:

AML	Anti-Money Laundering
CCAB	Consultative Committee of Accountancy Bodies
DOTAS	Disclosure of Tax Avoidance Schemes
GAAP	Generally Accepted Accounting Principles
GAAR	General Anti-Abuse Rule in Finance Act 2013
GDPR	General Data Protection Regulation
HMRC	Her Majesty's Revenue and Customs
MTD	Making Tax Digital
MLRO	Money Laundering Reporting Officer
NCA	National Crime Agency (previously the Serious Organised Crime Agency, SOCA)
POTAS	Promoters of Tax Avoidance Schemes
PCRT	Professional Conduct in Relation to Taxation
SRN	Scheme Reference Number

2. Fundamental principles

Overview of the fundamental principles

1. Ethical behaviour in the tax profession is critical. The work carried out by a member needs to be trusted by society at large as well as by clients and other stakeholders. What a member does reflects not just on themselves but on the profession as a whole.

2. A member must comply with the following fundamental principles:

Integrity
To be straightforward and honest in all professional and business relationships.

Objectivity
To not allow bias, conflict of interest or undue influence of others to override professional or business judgements.

Professional competence and due care
To maintain professional knowledge and skill at the level required to ensure that a client or employer receives competent professional service based on current developments in practice, legislation and techniques and act diligently and in accordance with applicable technical and professional standards.

Confidentiality
To respect the confidentiality of information acquired as a result of professional and business relationships and, therefore, not disclose any such information to third parties without proper and specific authority, unless there is a legal or professional right or duty to disclose, nor use the information for the personal advantage of the member or third parties.

Professional behaviour
To comply with relevant laws and regulations and avoid any action that discredits the profession.

3. PCRT Help sheet A: Submission of tax information and 'Tax filings'

Definition of filing of tax information and tax filings (filing)

1. For the purposes of this guidance, the term 'filing' includes any online submission of data, online filing or other filing that is prepared on behalf of the client for the purposes of disclosing to any taxing authority details that are to be used in the calculation of tax due by a client or a refund of tax due to the client or for other official purposes. It includes all taxes, NIC and duties.

2. A letter, or online notification, giving details in respect of a filing or as an amendment to a filing including, for example, any voluntary disclosure of an error should be dealt with as if it was a filing.

Making Tax Digital and filing

3. Tax administration systems, including the UK's, are increasingly moving to mandatory digital filing of tax information and returns.

4. Except in exceptional circumstances, a member will explicitly file in their capacity as agent. A member is advised to use the facilities provided for agents and to avoid knowing or using the client's personal access credentials.

5. A member should keep their access credentials safe from unauthorised use and consider periodic change of passwords.

6. A member is recommended to forward suspicious emails to phishing@hmrc.gsi.gov.uk and then delete them. It is also important to avoid clicking on websites or links in suspicious emails, or opening attachments.

7. Firms should have policies on cyber security, AML and GDPR.

Taxpayer's responsibility

8. The taxpayer has primary responsibility to submit correct and complete filings to the best of their knowledge and belief. The final decision as to whether to disclose any issue is that of the client but in relation to your responsibilities see paragraph 12 below.

9. In annual self-assessment returns or returns with short filing periods the filing may include reasonable estimates where necessary.

Member's responsibility

10. A member who prepares a filing on behalf of a client is responsible to the client for the accuracy of the filing based on the information provided.

11. In dealing with HMRC in relation to a client's tax affairs a member should bear in mind their duty of confidentiality to the client and that they are acting as the agent of their client. They have a duty to act in the best interests of their client.

12. A member should act in good faith in dealings with HMRC in accordance with the fundamental principle of integrity. In particular the member should take reasonable care and exercise appropriate professional scepticism when making statements or asserting facts on behalf of a client.

13. Where acting as a tax agent, a member is not required to audit the figures in the books and records provided or verify information provided by a client or by a third party. However, a member should take care not to be associated with the presentation of facts they know or believe to be incorrect or misleading, not to assert tax positions in a tax filing which they consider to have no sustainable basis.

14. When a member is communicating with HMRC, they should consider whether they need to make it clear to what extent they are relying on information which has been supplied by the client or a third party.

Materiality

15. Whether an amount is to be regarded as material depends upon the facts and circumstances of each case.

16. The profits of a trade, profession, vocation or property business should be computed in accordance with GAAP subject to any adjustment required or authorised by law in computing profits for those purposes. This permits a trade, profession, vocation or property business to disregard non-material adjustments in computing its accounting profits.

17. The application of GAAP, and therefore materiality does not extend beyond the accounting profits. Thus, the accounting concept of materiality cannot be applied when completing tax filings.

18. It should be noted that for certain small businesses an election may be made to use the cash basis instead; for small property businesses the default position is the cash basis. Where the cash basis is used, materiality is not relevant.

Disclosure

19. If a client is unwilling to include in a tax filing the minimum information required by law, the member should follow the guidance in Help sheet C: Dealing with Errors. The paragraphs below (paras 20 – 24) give guidance on some of the more common areas of uncertainty over disclosure.

20. In general, it is likely to be in a client's own interests to ensure that factors relevant to their tax liability are adequately disclosed to HMRC because:

    - their relationship with HMRC is more likely to be on a satisfactory footing if they can demonstrate good faith in their dealings with them. HMRC notes in 'Your Charter' that 'We want to give you a service that is fair, accurate and based on mutual trust and respect'
    - they will reduce the risk of a discovery or further assessment and may reduce exposure to interest and penalties.

21. It may be advisable to consider fuller disclosure than is strictly necessary. Reference to 'The Standards for Tax Planning' in PCRT may be relevant. The factors involved in making this decision include:
    - a filing relies on a valuation
    - the terms of the applicable law
    - the view taken by the member
    - the extent of any doubt that exists
    - the manner in which disclosure is to be made
    - the size and gravity of the item in question.

22. When advocating fuller disclosure than is necessary a member should ensure that their client is adequately aware of the issues involved and their potential implications. Fuller disclosure should only be made with the client's consent.

7

23. Cases will arise where there is doubt as to the correct treatment of an item of income or expenditure, or the computation of a gain or allowance. In such cases a member ought to consider what additional disclosure, if any, might be necessary. For example, additional disclosure should be considered where:

- there is inherent doubt as to the correct treatment of an item, for example, expenditure on repairs which might be regarded as capital in whole or part, or the VAT liability of a particular transaction, or
- HMRC has published its interpretation or has indicated its practice on a point, but the client proposes to adopt a different view, whether or not supported by Counsel's opinion. The member should refer to the guidance on the Veltema case and the paragraph below. See also HMRC guidance.

24. A member who is uncertain whether their client should disclose a particular item or of its treatment should consider taking further advice before reaching a decision. They should use their best endeavours to ensure that the client understands the issues, implications and the proposed course of action. Such a decision may have to be justified at a later date, so the member's files should contain sufficient evidence to support the position taken, including timely notes of discussions with the client and/or with other advisors, copies of any second opinion obtained and the client's final decision. A failure to take reasonable care may result in HMRC imposing a penalty if an error is identified after an enquiry.

Supporting documents

25. For the most part, HMRC does not consider that it is necessary for a taxpayer to provide supporting documentation in order to satisfy the taxpayer's overriding need to make a correct filing. HMRC's view is that, where it is necessary for that purpose, explanatory information should be entered in the 'white space' provided on the filing. However, HMRC does recognise that the taxpayer may wish to supply further details of a particular computation or transaction in order to minimise the risk of a discovery assessment being raised at a later time. Following the uncertainty created by the decision in Veltema, HMRC's guidance can be found in SP1/06 – Self Assessment: Finality and Discovery.

26. Further HMRC guidance says that sending attachments with a tax filing is intended for those cases where the taxpayer 'feels it is crucial to provide additional information to support the filing but for some reason cannot utilise the white space'.

Reliance on HMRC published guidance

27. Whilst it is reasonable in most circumstances to rely on HMRC published guidance, a member should be aware that the Tribunal and the courts will apply the law even if this conflicts with HMRC guidance.

28. Notwithstanding this, if a client has relied on HMRC guidance which is clear and unequivocal and HMRC resiles from any of the terms of the guidance, a Judicial Review claim is a possible route to pursue.

Approval of tax filings

29. The member should advise the client to review their tax filing before it is submitted.

30. The member should draw the client's attention to the responsibility which the client is taking in approving the filing as correct and complete. Attention should be drawn to any judgmental areas or positions reflected in the filing to ensure that the client is aware of these and their implications before they approve the filing.

31. A member should obtain evidence of the client's approval of the filing in electronic or non-electronic form.

4. PCRT Help sheet B: Tax advice

The Standards for Tax Planning

1. The Standards for Tax Planning are critical to any planning undertaken by members. They are:

   - Client Specific

     Tax planning must be specific to the particular client's facts and circumstances. Clients must be alerted to the wider risks and implications of any courses of action.

   - Lawful

     At all times members must act lawfully and with integrity and expect the same from their clients. Tax planning should be based on a realistic assessment of the facts and on a credible view of the law.

     Members should draw their client's attention to where the law is materially uncertain, for example because HMRC is known to take a different view of the law. Members should consider taking further advice appropriate to the risks and circumstances of the particular case, for example where litigation is likely.

   - Disclosure and transparency

     Tax advice must not rely for its effectiveness on HMRC having less than the relevant facts. Any disclosure must fairly represent all relevant facts.

   - Tax planning arrangements

     Members must not create, encourage or promote tax planning arrangements or structures that i) set out to achieve results that are contrary to the clear intention of Parliament in enacting relevant legislation and/or ii) are highly artificial or highly contrived and seek to exploit shortcomings within the relevant legislation.

   - Professional judgement and appropriate documentation

   - Applying these requirements to particular client advisory situations requires members to exercise professional judgement on a number of matters. Members should keep notes on a timely basis of the rationale for the judgements exercised in seeking to adhere to these requirements

Guidance

2. The paragraphs below provide guidance for members when considering whether advice complies with the Fundamental Principles and Standards for Tax Planning.

Tax evasion

3. A member should never be knowingly involved in tax evasion, although, of course, it is appropriate to act for a client who is rectifying their affairs.

Tax planning and advice

4. In contrast to tax evasion, tax planning is legal. However, under the Standard members 'must not create, encourage or promote tax planning arrangements that (i) set out to achieve results that are contrary to the clear intention of Parliament in enacting relevant legislation and/or (ii) are highly artificial or highly contrived and seek to exploit shortcomings within the relevant legislation'.

5. Things to consider:

   - have you checked that your engagement letter fully covers the scope of the planning advice?
   - have you taken the Standards for Tax Planning and the Fundamental Principles into account? Is it client specific? Is it lawful? Will all relevant facts be disclosed to HMRC? Is it creating, encouraging or promoting tax planning contrary to the 4th Standard for Tax Planning?
   - how tax sophisticated is the client?
   - has the client made clear what they wish to achieve by the planning?
   - what are the issues involved with the implementation of the planning?
   - what are the risks associated with the planning and have you warned the client of them? For example:
     - the strength of the legal interpretation relied upon
     - the potential application of the GAAR
     - the implications for the client, including the obligations of the client in relation to their tax return, if the planning requires disclosure under DOTAS or DASVOIT and the potential for an accelerated payment notice or partner payment notice?
     - the reputational risk to the client and the member of the planning in the public arena
     - the stress, cost and wider personal or business implications to the client in the event of a prolonged dispute with HMRC. This may involve unwelcomed publicity, costs, expenses and loss of management time over a significant period
     - if the client tenders for government contracts, the potential impact of the proposed tax planning on tendering for and retaining public sector contracts
     - the risk of counteraction. This may occur before the planning is completed or potentially there may be retrospective counteraction at a later date
     - the risk of challenge by HMRC. Such challenge may relate to the legal interpretation relied upon, but may alternatively relate to the construction of the facts, including the implementation of the planning
     - the risk and inherent uncertainty of litigation. The probability of the planning being overturned by the courts if litigated and the potential ultimate downside should the client be unsuccessful
     - is a second opinion necessary/advisable?
   - are the arrangements in line with any applicable code of conduct or ethical guidelines or stances for example the Banking Code, and fit and proper tests for charity trustees and pension administrators?
   - are you satisfied that the client understands the planning proposed?
   - have you documented the advice given and the reasoning behind it?

5. PCRT Help sheet C: Dealing with errors

Introduction

1. For the purposes of this guidance, the term 'error' is intended to include all errors and mistakes whether they were made by the client, the member, HMRC or any other party involved in a client's tax affairs, and whether made innocently or deliberately.

2. During a member's relationship with the client, the member may become aware of possible errors in the client's tax affairs. Unless the client is already aware of the possible error, they should be informed as soon as the member identifies them.

3. Where the error has resulted in the client paying too much tax the member should advise the client to make a repayment claim. The member should advise the client of the time limits to make a claim and have regard to any relevant time limits. The rest of this Help sheet deals with situations where tax may be due to HMRC.

4. Sometimes an error made by HMRC may mean that the client has not paid tax actually due or they have been incorrectly repaid tax. There may be fee costs as a result of correcting such mistakes. A member should bear in mind that, in some circumstances, clients or agents may be able to claim for additional professional costs incurred and compensation from HMRC.

5. A member should act correctly from the outset. A member should keep sufficient appropriate records of discussions and advice and when dealing with errors the member should:
   - give the client appropriate advice
   - if necessary, so long as they continue to act for the client, seek to persuade the client to behave correctly
   - take care not to appear to be assisting a client to plan or commit any criminal offence or to conceal any offence which has been committed
   - in appropriate situations, or where in doubt, discuss the client's situation with a colleague or an independent third party (having due regard to client confidentiality).

6. Once aware of a possible error, a member must bear in mind the legislation on money laundering and the obligations and duties which this places upon them.

7. Where the member may have made the error, the member should consider whether they need to notify their professional indemnity insurers.

8. In any situation where a member has concerns about their own position, they should consider taking specialist legal advice. For example, where a client appears to have used the member to assist in the commissioning of a criminal offence and people could question whether the member had acted honestly in in good faith. Note that The Criminal Finances Act 2017 has created new criminal offences of failure to prevent facilitation of tax evasion.

9. The flowchart below summarises the recommended steps a member should take where a possible error arises. It must be read in conjunction with the guidance and commentary that follow it.

Dealing with errors flowchart

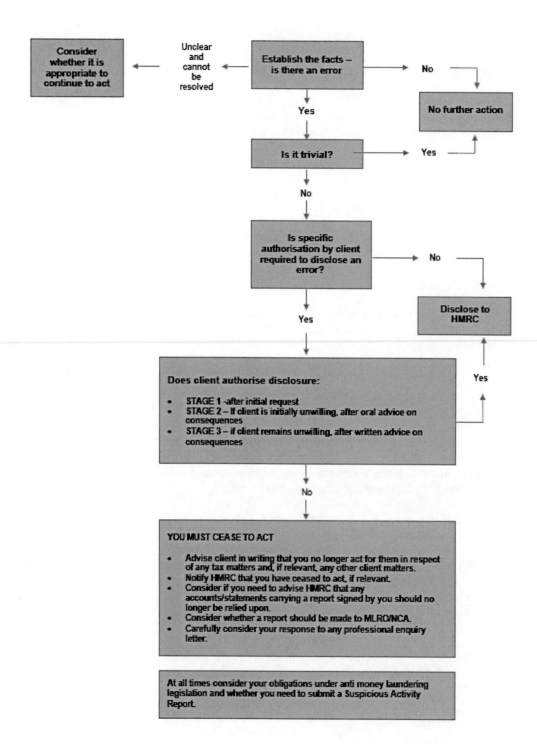

AAT is a registered charity. No. 1050724

6. PCRT Help sheet D: Requests for data by HMRC

Introduction

1. For the purposes of this help sheet the term 'data' includes documents in whatever form (including electronic) and other information. While this guidance relates to HMRC requests, other government bodies or organisations may also approach the member for data. The same principles apply.

2. A distinction should be drawn between a request for data made informally ('informal requests') and those requests for data which are made in exercise of a power to require the provision of the data requested ('formal requests').

3. Similarly, requests addressed to a client and those addressed to a member require different handling.

4. Where a member no longer acts for a client, the member remains subject to the duty of confidentiality. In relation to informal requests, the member should refer the enquirer either to the former client or if authorised by the client to the new agent. In relation to formal requests addressed to the member, the termination of their professional relationship with the client does not affect the member's duty to comply with that request, where legally required to do so.

5. A member should comply with formal requests and should not seek to frustrate legitimate requests for information. Adopting a constructive approach may help to resolve issues promptly and minimise costs to all parties.

6. Whilst a member should be aware of HMRC's powers it may be appropriate to take specialist advice.

7. Devolved tax authorities have separate powers.

8. Two flowcharts are at the end of this help sheet:
   - requests for data addressed to the member
   - requests for data addressed to the client.

Informal requests addressed to the client

9. From time to time, HMRC chooses to communicate directly with clients rather than with the appointed agent.

10. HMRC has given reassurances that it is working to ensure that initial contact on compliance checks will normally be via the agent and only if the agent does not reply within an appropriate timescale will the contact be directly with the client.

11. When the member assists a client in dealing with such requests from HMRC, the member should advise the client that cooperation with informal requests can provide greater opportunities for the taxpayer to find a pragmatic way to work through the issue at hand with HMRC.

Informal requests addressed to the member

12. Disclosure in response to informal requests can only be made with the client's permission.

13. In many instances, the client will have authorised routine disclosure of relevant data, for example, through the engagement letter. However, if there is any doubt about whether the client has authorised disclosure, the member should ask the client to approve what is to be disclosed.

14. Where an oral enquiry is made by HMRC, a member should consider asking for it to be put in writing so that a response may be agreed with the client.

15. Although there is no obligation to comply with an informal request in whole or in part, a member should advise the client whether it is in the client's best interests to disclose such data, as lack of cooperation may have a direct impact on penalty negotiations post—enquiry.

16. Informal requests may be forerunners to formal requests compelling the disclosure of data. Consequently, it may be sensible to comply with such requests.

Formal requests addressed to the client

17. In advising their client a member should consider whether specialist advice may be needed, for example on such issues as whether the notice has been issued in accordance with the relevant tax legislation and whether the data request is valid.

18. The member should also advise the client about any relevant right of appeal against the formal request if appropriate and of the consequences of a failure to comply.

19. If the notice is legally effective the client is legally obliged to comply with the request.

20. The most common statutory notice issued to clients and third parties by HMRC is under Schedule 36 FA 2008.

Formal requests addressed to the member

21. The same principles apply to formal requests to the member as formal requests to clients.

22. If a formal request is valid it **overrides the member's duty of confidentiality** to their client. The member is therefore obliged to comply with the request. Failure to comply with their legal obligations can expose the member to civil or criminal penalties.

23. In cases where the member is not legally precluded by the terms of the notice from communicating with the client, the member should advise the client of the notice and keep the client informed of progress and developments.

24. The member should ensure that in complying with any notice they do not provide information or data outside the scope of the notice.

25. If a member is faced with a situation in which HMRC is seeking to enforce disclosure by the removal of data, or seeking entrance to inspect business premises occupied by a member in their capacity as an adviser, the member should consider seeking immediate professional advice, to ensure that this is the legally correct course of action.

Privileged data

26. Legal privilege arises under common law and may only be overridden if this is set out in legislation. It protects a party's right to communicate in confidence with a legal adviser. The privilege belongs to the client and not to the member.

27. If a document is privileged: The client cannot be required to make disclosure of that document to HMRC. Another party cannot disclose it (including the member), without the client's express permission.

28. There are two types of legal privilege under common law: legal advice privilege and litigation privilege.

(a) Legal advice privilege

Covers documents passing between a client and their legal adviser prepared for the purposes of obtaining or giving legal advice. However, communications from a tax adviser who is not a practising lawyer will not attract legal advice privilege even if such individuals are giving advice on legal matters such as tax law.

(b) Litigation privilege

Covers data created for the dominant purpose of litigation. Litigation privilege may arise where litigation has not begun, but is merely contemplated and may apply to data prepared by non-lawyer advisors (including tax advisors). There are two important limits on litigation privilege. First, it does not arise in respect of non- adversarial proceedings. Second, the documents must be produced for the 'dominant purpose' of litigation.

29. A privilege under Schedule 36 paragraphs 19, (documents relating to the conduct of a pending appeal), 24 and 25 (auditors, and tax advisors' documents) might exist by "quasi-privilege" and if this is the case a tax adviser does not have to provide those documents. Care should be taken as not all data may be privileged.

30. A member who receives a request for data, some of which the member believes may be subject to privilege or 'quasi-privilege', should take independent legal advice on the position, unless expert in this area.

Help sheet D: Flowchart regarding requests for data by HMRC to the Member

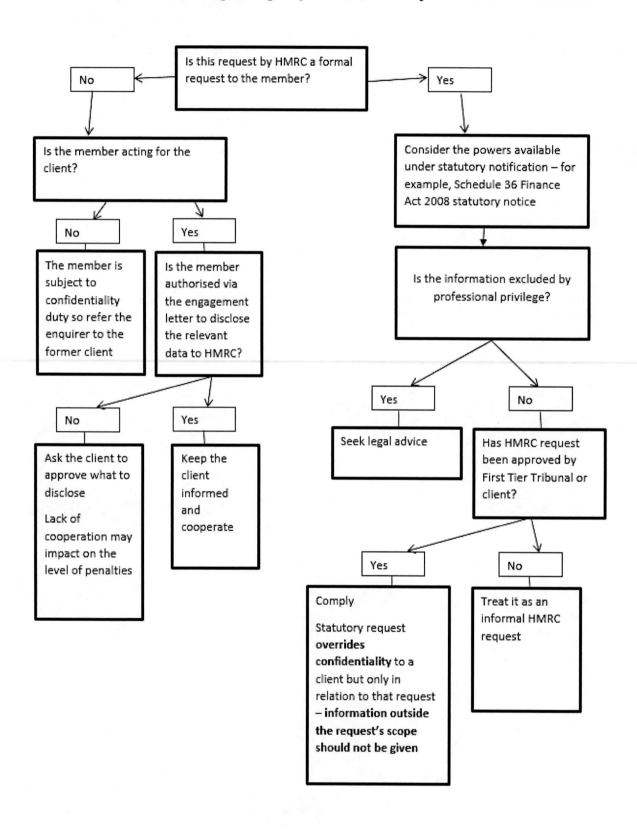

Is this request by HMRC a formal request to the member?

No

Is the member acting for the client?

No — The member is subject to confidentiality duty so refer the enquirer to the former client

Yes — Is the member authorised via the engagement letter to disclose the relevant data to HMRC?

No — Ask the client to approve what to disclose

Lack of cooperation may impact on the level of penalties

Yes — Keep the client informed and cooperate

Yes

Consider the powers available under statutory notification – for example, Schedule 36 Finance Act 2008 statutory notice

Is the information excluded by professional privilege?

Yes — Seek legal advice

No — Has HMRC request been approved by First Tier Tribunal or client?

Yes — Comply

Statutory request **overrides confidentiality** to a client but only in relation to that request **– information outside the request's scope should not be given**

No — Treat it as an informal HMRC request

Help sheet D: Flowchart regarding requests for data by HMRC to the Client

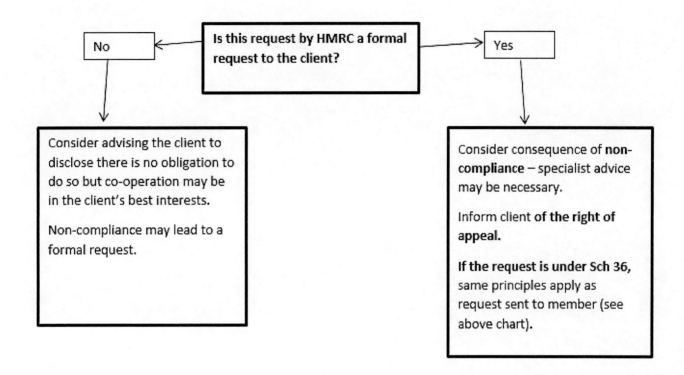

| No | Is this request by HMRC a formal request to the client? | Yes |

No path:

Consider advising the client to disclose there is no obligation to do so but co-operation may be in the client's best interests.

Non-compliance may lead to a formal request.

Yes path:

Consider consequence of **non-compliance** – specialist advice may be necessary.

Inform client **of the right of appeal.**

If the request is under Sch 36, same principles apply as request sent to member (see above chart).

The Association of Accounting Technicians
140 Aldersgate Street
London
EC1A 4HY
t: +44 (0)20 7397 3000
f: +44 (0)20 7397 3009
e: aat@aat.org.uk
aat.org.uk

Section 1

PRACTICE QUESTIONS

PRINCIPLES AND RULES UNDERPINNING TAX

1   MICROMATTERS LTD

(a)   You are employed by a firm of accountants. Your firm has received a formal (legal) request for information from HM Revenue and Customs in relation to Micromatters Ltd, one of the firm's clients.

Using the AAT guidelines 'Professional conduct in relation to taxation', explain your responsibilities in relation to this matter.

(b)   You are employed by a firm of accountants. Your firm has received an informal request for information from HM Revenue and Customs in relation to a former client of the firm.

Using the AAT guidelines 'Professional conduct in relation to taxation', explain your responsibilities in relation to this matter.

2   CORA

(a)   You work for a firm of accountants. You have seen a report in the local newspaper concerning Cora, a client of your firm. The report concerned the recent sale of a painting for £410,000. The report claimed that the painting was owned by Cora for many years until she sold it to the current vendor on 1 May 2019. There is no mention in Cora's 2019/20 tax return of a painting being sold.

Using the AAT guidelines 'Professional conduct in relation to taxation', explain your responsibilities in relation to this matter.

(b)   A potential client, Nisha, has approached the firm of accountants where you work. Nisha has rented out a property for two years without disclosing the income to HMRC. Nisha now wants to make the disclosure to HMRC with your assistance.

Using the AAT guidelines 'Professional conduct in relation to taxation', explain whether your firm could engage Nisha as a client, given the non-disclosure of income.

3 TOM

(a) Tom has been a client of your firm for a number of years. You have recently discovered that Tom has omitted to include the income received from his Irish rental property in his income tax return. When you contact Tom to discuss this he has refused to make any amendments stating that any errors in the tax return are not his problem.

Using the AAT guidelines 'Professional conduct in relation to taxation', explain the respective responsibilities of your firm and Tom in relation to his tax return.

(b) Your manager has suggested that Tom's attitude suggests the possibility of tax evasion here.

Explain the meaning of the terms 'tax evasion', 'tax avoidance' and 'tax planning' and whether the firm can be involved with returns involving evidence of each.

4 SOFIA

(a) Sofia is a manager in the accountancy firm you work at. She has developed a tax planning scheme that she believes can reduce the tax liabilities of a number of clients in your firm. She has been discussing it with other employees in the office and believes it will be highly profitable as it can be used for many taxpayers without adjustments. The scheme relies on an interpretation of tax legislation that has not yet been provided in Court, however HMRC have already indicated that they do not prescribe to this interpretation.

Using the AAT guidelines 'Professional Conduct in relation to taxation', explain the impact of the Standards for Tax Planning, in relation to this scheme.

(b) The accountancy firm where you work has recently won a new client who is worried about data security if you file her income tax return online. She does not want to give you any of her personal passwords.

Using the AAT guidelines 'Professional Conduct in relation to taxation', explain the actions your firm should take to keep the client's data confidential when filing online.

5 TAX PRINCIPLES

(a) A government wants to use the tax system to encourage active lifestyles. It has proposed that companies whose employees walk a certain number of steps during the working day should be entitled to tax relief.

The companies would have to provide their employees with devices to log the number of steps walked, and then enter this data into a government website on a weekly basis.

The tax relief is in the form of a tax credit paid back to the company, of an amount based on the company's profit. It is given if at least 100 employees walk at least 20,000 steps each, at least four times each week.

Identify and explain TWO principles underpinning the tax system which would not apply to this proposal.

(b) A tax system may be progressive, regressive or proportional.

Define each of the terms 'progressive tax', 'regressive tax', and 'proportional tax'.

6   CLARISSA

(a)   Clarissa is one of the clients at the accountancy firm where you work. Your manager Duncan has already worked out that Clarissa is not automatically non-UK resident nor automatically UK resident for 2021/22. Duncan tells you Clarissa has three ties to the UK in 2021/22.

State the TWO further pieces of information you need to know about Clarissa to work out whether she is UK resident in 2021/22 and explain the implications of the information.

(b)   Lewis is a client of your firm. He is resident in the UK but is non-UK domiciled. Your manager wants you to warn Lewis that he may have UK deemed domicile.

Explain the TWO scenarios in which Lewis would have UK deemed domicile.

7   JOSEPH

(a)   You work for a firm of accountants. Joseph, one of your clients, is UK resident but is not UK domiciled, nor deemed domicile.

Explain the effect of both Joseph's residence status and domicile status on his liability to income tax.

(b)   Colette is a high-profile client of the accountancy firm where you work. She currently has adjusted net income of just over £100,000. Your manager has suggested that if Colette were to make a small charitable donation, this would increase her available personal allowance and save tax, as well as help the charity Colette supports. Colette is concerned about her public image if she is seen to be taking part in tax avoidance.

Explain the difference between tax avoidance and tax planning in respect of the charitable donation.

INCOME FROM EMPLOYMENT

8   SNAPE

(a)   Snape and Sam were provided with company cars by their employers throughout the tax year 2021/22.

	Snape	Sam
Car registration date	1 July 2020	1 October 2019
Emissions g/km	129	129
Fuel type	Diesel	Diesel
RDE2 standard met?	No	No
List price	£21,995	£27,000
Cost of car to employer	£21,000	£23,000
Annual running costs	£3,500	£1,370
Annual fuel costs	£2,000	£2,000
Percentage private use	65%	25%
Private fuel provided?	Yes	Yes
Employee contribution to private fuel	£50 per month	£0

Calculate the relevant percentage, the car benefit, and the fuel benefit for Snape and Sam for the tax year 2021/22. Round your benefit amounts to the nearest pound (£).

	Snape	Sam
Percentage (%)		
Car benefit £		
Fuel benefit £		

(b)   Calculate the taxable benefit provided to the employee in each scenario below for the tax year 2021/22. Round your benefit amounts to the nearest pound (£).

Scenarios	£
On 6 December 2021, Loach was provided with a company loan for £7,000 on which he pays interest at 1.4% per annum.	
Swift plc purchased a property for £100,000 in December 2015. In May 2016 the company spent £30,000 on an extension to the property. On 1 November 2020 an employee, Margarita, occupied the property. The market value of the property on 1 November 2020 was £220,000. The annual value of the property was £1,000.	
Eve was provided with a flat (which was not job related) by her employer. The flat has an annual value of £6,000 and Eve's employer pays rent of £450 per month. Eve pays £100 per month towards the private use of the flat.	

(c)   Read the following statements and tick the appropriate box to indicate whether they are true or false.

	True	False
Dan is provided with furniture by his employer. Dan is taxed on 25% of the market value per annum.		
Evan is provided with workplace childcare for his son. This is an exempt benefit.		
A loan of £12,000 provided to Frances in order that she can buy items wholly, exclusively and necessarily for her employment is exempt from income tax		
Gerri will not be taxed on the reimbursement of expenses for her home to work travel.		
Harry is provided with an eye test and spectacles for VDU use which are exempt benefits.		

9   FRODO

(a)   Frodo was provided with a company car by his employer on 5 August 2021.

	Frodo
Car registration date	4 August 2021
Emissions g/km	112
Fuel type	Petrol
List price	£26,000
Cost of car to employer	£24,000
Frodo's contribution to private use of the car	£70 per month
Private fuel provided?	Yes
Frodo's contribution to private fuel	£30 per month

Calculate the relevant percentage, the car benefit, and the fuel benefit for Frodo for the tax year 2021/22. Round your benefit amounts to the nearest pound (£).

	Frodo
Percentage (%)	
Car benefit £	
Fuel benefit £	

(b)   **Calculate the taxable benefit provided to the employee in each scenario below for the tax year 2021/22. Round your benefit amounts to the nearest pound (£).**

Scenarios	£
On 2 June 2021 Yousef was provided by his employer with a laptop computer costing £750 for private use.	
On 4 August 2021 Ian was provided by his employer with a van with a list price of £12,000 for private use. The van has zero CO_2 emissions. Ian is not provided with any private fuel.	
On 6 April 2021 Siti left her employment. She took up the offer of purchasing a camera for £200 which she had been lent by her employer several years previously. This camera cost the company £500 and up to the end of the tax year 2020/21 Siti had been taxed on taxable benefits totalling £350. The camera was worth £250 at 6 April 2021.	
Angel was provided with job related accommodation throughout the tax year 2021/22. This house cost her employers £125,000 in June 2019. The house has an annual value of £2,250. Angel's employer provided her with furniture at a cost of £10,000 and paid for the electricity bill which cost £1,200. Angel earns a salary of £22,000 for the tax year 2021/22.	
Since 1 August 2021, Esme has lived in a house provided by her employer. This house cost her employers £175,000 in June 2014. The house has an annual value of £3,250 and Esme contributes £100 per month towards the cost of the benefit. The property had a market value of £228,000 when Esme moved in.	

(c)   **Identify whether each of the following statements about benefits is true or false.**

Tick one box on each line.

	True	False
The provision of a car parking space in a multi-storey car park near the place of work is an exempt benefit.		
Free daily lunches provided to staff who have worked for the company for at least seven years are exempt benefits.		
The provision of a workplace nursery at the workplace is an exempt benefit.		
An interest free loan of £9,000 is made on 6 April 2021 and written off on 5 April 2022. The write off of loan is an exempt benefit.		

10   BARRY

(a)   Barry and Crouch were provided by their employers with company cars, which were still being used at 5 April 2022.

	Barry	Crouch
Car registration date	1 December 2019	1 August 2021
Date provided to employee	1 January 2021	1 September 2021
Emissions g/km	126	102
Private use percentage	10%	80%
Fuel type	Diesel	Petrol
RDE2 standard met?	No	N/a
List price	£27,000	£20,000
Cost of car to employer	£25,000	£20,000
Annual running costs paid by company other than fuel	£1,650	£1,370
Private fuel provided?	No	Yes
Annual total fuel cost	£5,000	£5,000
Employee contribution to purchase of car	£6,000	£0
Employee contribution to running costs	£50 per month	£0
Employee contribution to private fuel	N/a	£1,000

Calculate the relevant percentage, the car benefit, and the fuel benefit for Barry and Crouch for the tax year 2021/22. Round your benefit amounts to the nearest pound (£).

	Barry	Crouch
Percentage (%)		
Car benefit £		
Fuel benefit £		

(b) **Calculate the taxable benefit provided to the employee in each scenario below for the tax year 2021/22. Round your benefit amounts to the nearest pound (£).**

Scenarios	£
On 6 October 2021 Nikita was provided with a company loan of £28,000 on which she pays interest at 0.75% per annum.	
Percy's employer provides him with a van for private use. The van has a market value of £20,000 and CO$_2$ emissions of 130g/km. Percy is not provided with any fuel for private use. Percy has the use of the van throughout the tax year 2021/22.	
Molly was provided with a house (which is not job related) by her employer for the whole of the tax year 2021/22. The house has an annual value of £5,000 and cost Molly's employer £150,000 in September 2020. The house contains furniture costing £40,000. Heating bills of £750 per year are paid by her employer. Molly pays £200 per month towards the private use of the house.	

(c) **Read the following statements about benefits and tick the appropriate box to indicate whether they are true or false.**

Tick one box on each line.

	True	False
The payment of £800 fees for office employees attending computer skills courses is an exempt benefit.		
An employer pays £500 for a smart phone for an employee. The employee will be taxed on this amount.		
Long service awards of £500 cash are given to employees completing 20 years' service. The employees will not be taxed on these awards.		
Health screenings for employees every six months. All health screenings are exempt benefits.		

11 JACKIE

(a) Jackie was provided with a company car by her employer which she still used at 5 April 2022.

	Jackie
Car registration date	30 April 2021
Date car provided to Jackie	1 May 2021
Dates car unavailable due to accidents – no replacement car provided	1-14 August 2021 inclusive 1-21 October 2021 inclusive
Emissions g/km	102
Fuel type	Diesel
RDE2 standard met?	No
List price	£12,400
Cost of car to employer	£10,000
Optional accessories fitted to car after delivery	£1,500
Jackie's contributions for use of car	£0
Private fuel provided?	Yes
Private fuel cost	£2,000
Jackie's contribution towards cost of private fuel	£2,000

Calculate the relevant percentage, the car benefit, and the fuel benefit for Jackie for the tax year 2021/22. Round your benefit amounts to the nearest pound (£).

	Jackie
Percentage (%)	
Car benefit £	
Fuel benefit £	

(b) **Calculate the taxable benefit provided to the employee in each scenario below for the tax year 2021/22. Round your benefit amounts to the nearest pound (£).**

Scenarios	£
Gibbs is provided with accommodation by his employer, Tallmark plc. The property cost Tallmark plc £250,000 in May 2018 and the company spent £45,000 on improvements in June 2021. The property has an annual value of £6,500 and Gibbs pays rent of £150 per month to Tallmark plc. The property had a market value of £265,000 when Gibbs moved in on 20 December 2018.	
Diego is provided with a house by his employer. The accommodation benefit is £2,600 before taking account of the following expenditure. The property was furnished by his employer at a cost of £20,000. The employer also paid for regular gardening and cleaning at the property which cost a total of £2,100 for the tax year 2021/22. In addition the employer spent £5,600 during the tax year 2021/22 on extending the garage.	
During the tax year 2021/22 Betsy receives a £100 payment under her employer's staff suggestion scheme in respect of a proposal she made that reduced the costs incurred by the business. Her employer also pays her home telephone bills of £400 even though Betsy has no business use of the telephone.	
Bismah's employer moved to larger premises which have a staff canteen available to all staff. Bismah is entitled to subsidised meals in the canteen for which she paid £1 per day for 250 days. The meals cost her employer £480 to provide.	
Althea's employer made an interest-free loan to her of £16,000 on 1 April 2021. On 30 June 2021 Althea repaid £4,000 of the loan. Althea uses the average method of assessment.	

(c) **Indicate whether each of the following statements about taxable benefits is true or false.**

Tick one box on each line.

	True	False
Arthur receives a mobile telephone for business and private use from his employer. Arthur is taxed on the private use portion of the costs.		
Brick Ltd provides a pool car at its factory for use by employees to travel around the site. This is an exempt benefit.		
Colin is allowed use of a company van for a fortnight's camping holiday. There is no other private use. This is an exempt benefit.		

12   SID

(a)   Sid was provided with a company car by his employer from May 2019 until he left employment on 1 December 2021.

	Sid
Car registration date	1 May 2019
Emissions g/km	136
Fuel type	Diesel
RDE2 standard met?	Yes
List price	£30,000
Cost of car to employer	£29,400
Sid's contributions for use of car	£20 per month
Private fuel provided?	Yes
Sid's contribution towards cost of private fuel	£0

Calculate the relevant percentage, the car benefit, and the fuel benefit for Sid for the tax year 2021/22. Round your benefit amounts to the nearest pound (£).

	Sid
Percentage (%)	
Car benefit £	
Fuel benefit £	

(b)   **Calculate the taxable benefit provided to the employee in each scenario below for the tax year 2021/22. Round your benefit amounts to the nearest pound (£).**

Scenarios	£
On 6 October 2021, Bharat was provided with a loan of a home cinema system worth £3,600 by his employer. The cinema system is only used for private purposes.	
Sybil was provided with a flat (which is not job related) by her employer. The flat has an annual value of £5,600 and Sybil's employer pays rent of £420 per month. Sybil pays £80 per month towards the private use of the flat.	
Ben works for HF Ltd which provides its employees with fitness facilities on the company premises. The facilities are only open to employees. The annual running cost of the gym is £450 per employee. Ben uses the facilities once each week throughout the tax year the tax year 2021/22.	
Bim's employer pays for his annual subscription at a health club near Bim's home. The subscription costs the employer £450 per annum.	

(c) **Indicate whether each of the following statements about benefits and expenses is true or false.**

Tick one box on each line.

	True	False
A payment of £500 to an employee in accordance with the rules of the staff suggestion scheme is an exempt benefit.		
Employees who work with computers can receive a free eye test organised by their employer, without being charged tax.		
The funding of a Christmas party of £100 per employee in the tax year is a taxable benefit.		
A donation to a UK political party by an employee is an allowable expense reducing employment income.		

13 JAYDEN

(a) Jayden was provided with a company car by his employer throughout the tax year 2021/22.

	Jayden
Car registration date	1 May 2020
Emissions g/km	46
Electric range (miles)	35
Fuel type	Petrol hybrid
List price	£37,000
Cost of car to employer	£36,000
Jayden's contributions towards the car purchase	£8,000
Private fuel provided?	No

Calculate the relevant percentage, the car benefit, and the fuel benefit for Jayden for the tax year 2021/22. Round your benefit amounts to the nearest pound (£).

	Jayden
Percentage (%)	
Car benefit £	
Fuel benefit £	

(b) **Calculate the taxable benefit provided to the employee in each scenario below for the tax year 2021/22. Round your benefit amounts to the nearest pound (£) and indicate an exempt benefit with a zero (0).**

Scenarios	£
Zamir is provided with a free annual health screening which costs the employer £350 per head.	
Yasmin attended the annual staff party which cost £220 per head.	
Graham received payments of £7 per night for 15 nights for personal expenses when staying away from home for work elsewhere in the UK.	
Bailey had to relocate to a new town when he was promoted. His employer paid his removal expenses of £12,000.	
When she was promoted to manager grade, Clare received a smart phone which cost her employer £380 per year.	

(c) **Indicate whether each of the following statements about benefits is true or false.**

Tick one box on each line.

	True	False
Sian was provided with accommodation by her employer three years after the property was purchased by the employer. The market value of the property is used to calculate the additional benefit.		
Jane received a non-cash long service award of £50 per year of service. The award is tax free.		
Ron uses his own car for business travelling. During the tax year 2021/22 he travelled 18,000 business miles for which he was paid 38p per mile by his employer. Ron can claim a tax allowable expense of £1,260.		

14   MARIO

(a)   Mario and Luke were provided by their employers with company cars, which were still being used at 5 April 2022.

	Mario	Luke
Car registration date	1 August 2015	1 January 2022
Date provided to employee	1 January 2020	5 January 2022
Emissions g/km	158	37
Electric range (miles)	N/a	75
Fuel type	Diesel	Petrol hybrid
RDE2 standard met?	No	N/a
List price	£32,000	£50,000
Private fuel provided?	Yes	No
Employee contribution to purchase of car	£0	£10,000
Employee contribution to running costs	£0	£10 per month
Employee contribution to private fuel	£0	N/a

Calculate the relevant percentage, the car benefit, and the fuel benefit for Mario and Luke for the tax year 2021/22. Round your benefit amounts to the nearest pound (£).

	Mario	Luke
Percentage (%)		
Car benefit £		
Fuel benefit £		

(b)   Calculate the taxable benefit provided to the employee in each scenario below for the tax year 2021/22. Round your benefit amounts to the nearest pound (£).

Scenarios	£
During the tax year 2021/22 Tilly used her own car for her employment, driving 25,000 business miles. Her employer paid her 50 pence per mile for this.	
Zoe's employer provided her with a van for private use, including private fuel. The van has a market value of £15,000 and CO_2 emissions of 140g/km. Zoe had the use of the van throughout the tax year the tax year 2021/22.	
Lola had an interest-free loan from her employer of £18,000 outstanding on 6 April 2021. Lola paid back the full amount on 6 January 2022.	
Jack was provided with a house (which is not job related) by his employer for the whole of the tax year 2021/22. The house has an annual value of £7,000 and cost Jack's employer £275,000 in February 2018 when it was first provided to Jack. An extension was built in January 2021 for £25,000. Jack pays £400 per month towards the private use of the house.	

(c)   Read the following statements about benefits and tick the appropriate box to indicate whether they are true or false.

Tick one box on each line.

	True	False
A car parking space provided at the company office for an employee is an exempt benefit.		
An employer provides an employee with private use of a TV with market value £2,000. The benefit for the employee is £2,000.		
Sue's employer provides her with two mobile phones – one for her and one for her husband. Sue is not taxed on the provision of the phones.		
Anne attends one staff party in the tax year 2021/22. The party cost her employer £100 per employee. This is a taxable benefit.		

INCOME FROM INVESTMENT AND PROPERTY

15   SOPHIE

(a)   In the tax year 2021/22 Sophie has dividend income of £4,700. £500 of this income falls into Sophie's higher rate band and the remainder falls into her additional rate band.

Calculate Sophie's income tax liability in respect of her dividend income in whole pounds.

In the tax year 2021/22 Serena has bank interest of £4,300 and lottery winnings of £200. Her non-savings taxable income, after personal allowance, is £35,600.

State the amount of Serena's taxable savings income.

Calculate Serena's income tax liability in respect of her savings income in whole pounds.

(b) Googoosh has two properties, details of which are given in the table.

Calculate the taxable income and the allowable expenses for each property in the tax year 2021/22. Enter 0 (zero) if the answer is nil.

Property	Letting and cost information	Taxable income £	Allowable expenses £
Flat	The furnished flat was let throughout the tax year 2021/22 with rent payable on the first of the month. The rent was £500 per month during 2021. On 1 January 2022 the rent was increased to £525 per month. Googoosh purchased a new corner sofa for the property for £1,800. A sofa similar to the old sofa would have cost £1,620. Googoosh was able to sell the old sofa for £130.		
House	The unfurnished house was rented out for £480 per month, payable on the 10th of the month, but was empty until 1 November 2021 when a family moved in on a twelve month lease.		

(c) **Identify whether each of the following statements about property income is true or false.**

Tick one box on each line.

	True	False
Giorgis has bought a house which he intends to let furnished. The initial cost of providing the furniture will be an allowable cost when calculating taxable property income.		
Income from property is always taxed on the cash basis unless the taxpayer elects to use the accruals basis.		

16 CASTILAS

(a) Castilas' only income for the tax year 2021/22 is dividend income of £18,000.

Calculate Castilas' income tax liability in respect of his dividend income in whole pounds.

Hannah received bank interest of £8,900 and interest on overpaid tax of £25 in the tax year 2021/22. Her other taxable income, after any available personal allowance, totalled £116,200.

State Hannah's taxable savings income.

Calculate the total income tax payable on this savings income by Hannah in whole pounds.

(b) Sunita has two properties, details of which are given in the table below. She has elected to be taxed on the accruals basis.

Calculate the taxable income and the allowable expenses for each property in the tax year 2021/22. Enter 0 (zero) if the answer is nil.

Property	Letting and cost information	Taxable income £	Allowable expenses £
House	The unfurnished house is rented out for £1,000 per month. The property was occupied until 1 September 2021 when the tenants suddenly moved out, owing the rent for August. Sunita knows she will not recover this rent. The property was let again from 1 December 2021. The rent is received on the first of each month. Sunita incurred 5% commission to the agent on rent received. This was deducted from each monthly rent payment.		
Flat	The furnished flat is rented out for £600 per month. The property was occupied by Sunita during April 2021. She then started looking for a tenant, but the property was unoccupied until 1 July when a couple moved in on a twelve-month lease. The rent was received on the 8th of each month. In May 2021, Sunita purchased new lounge furniture for the property for £2,000 and dining furniture for £1,200. Lounge furniture similar to the old furniture could have been purchased for £1,100. Sunita sold the old lounge furniture for £180. The property did not have any dining furniture prior to the purchase in May.		

(c) **Identify whether each of the following statements about investment income is true or false.**

Tick one box on each line.

	True	False
Property losses from furnished lettings can be deducted from profits on unfurnished lettings.		
Dividends received from an ISA are always exempt from tax.		

17   RAMOS

(a)   In the tax year 2021/22 Ramos received a dividend of £27,600. His other taxable income, after personal allowances, totalled £26,300.

   Calculate the amount of the dividends which are taxed at 7.5% in the tax year 2021/22.

   ┌─────────────────────────┐
   │   │
   └─────────────────────────┘

   In the tax year 2021/22 Pete received premium bond winnings of £3,000 and building society interest of £1,400. His other taxable income totalled £172,000.

   State Pete's taxable savings income the tax year 2021/22.

   ┌─────────────────────────┐
   │   │
   └─────────────────────────┘

   Calculate the income tax payable by Pete on this savings income in the tax year 2021/22 to the nearest pound.

   ┌─────────────────────────┐
   │   │
   └─────────────────────────┘

(b)   Will has two properties, details of which are given in the table below.

   Calculate the taxable income and the allowance expenses for each property in the tax year 2021/22. Enter 0 (zero) if the answer is nil.

Property	Letting and cost information	Taxable income £	Allowable expenses £
Cottage	The furnished cottage is rented out for £500 per month. All rent was received during the tax year. Will pays gardeners fees of £50 a month and cleaners bills of £70 a month. He also paid for repairs costing £400. All amounts were paid during the tax year, except for the last month's cleaner's fees.		
Flat	The furnished flat is rented out for £3,600 per year. The property was unoccupied until 1 July 2021. Rent is paid monthly in arrears. Will paid water rates of £500 and insurance of £500 in respect of the flat for 2021/22 in May 2021.		

(c)   **Identify whether each of the following statements about property income is true or false.**

   Tick one box on each line.

	True	False
When calculating an individual's property income any costs of improving the property are not allowable.		
Property losses can be offset against an individual's total income in the tax year.		

18   MARLON

(a)   In the tax year 2021/22 Marlon has dividend income of £3,300. £1,500 of this income is covered by Marlon's personal allowance and the remainder falls into his basic rate band.

Calculate Marlon's income tax liability in respect of his dividend income in whole pounds.

```
┌──────────────────────────────┐
│                              │
└──────────────────────────────┘
```

In the tax year 2021/22 Dean has building society interest of £8,300 and interest from an individual savings account of £700. Dean's non-savings income, after the personal allowance, is £70,000. Dean has no dividend income.

State Dean's taxable savings income the tax year 2021/22.

```
┌──────────────────────────────┐
│                              │
└──────────────────────────────┘
```

Calculate Dean's income tax liability in respect of his savings income in whole pounds.

```
┌──────────────────────────────┐
│                              │
└──────────────────────────────┘
```

(b)   Edward has two properties, details of which are given in the table below.

Calculate the taxable income and the allowance expenses for each property in the tax year 2021/22. Enter zero (0) if the answer is nil.

Property	Letting and cost information	Taxable income £	Allowable expenses £
House	The unfurnished house is rented out for £7,200 per annum, payable on the first of the month. The property was occupied until 28 February 2022 when the tenants suddenly moved out, without paying the rent for February. Edward moved in for the month of March before the property was let again from 1 April 2022 to another family. Edward paid £700 for council tax during the year.		
Bungalow	The furnished bungalow is rented out for £550 per month, receivable on the 6th of the month. The property was unoccupied until 6 October 2021. Edward purchased a new sofa for the property for £2,100. A sofa similar to the old one would have cost £900. Edward sold the old sofa for £220.		

(c) **Identify whether each of the following statements about taxable income is true or false.**

Tick one box on each line.

	True	False
Property expenses incurred when the property is empty cannot be deducted from property income, even if the property is available to let.		
In the tax year 2021/22 the maximum amount that Taran (aged 42) can invest in an ISA is £1,000.		

19   HUANG

(a)   In the tax year 2021/22 Michelle has dividend income of £2,600. All of this income falls into Michelle's higher rate band.

Calculate Michelle's income tax liability in respect of her dividend income in the tax year 2021/22 to the nearest pound.

In the tax year 2021/22 Huang received £7,700 made up of bank interest income of £5,700 and lottery winnings of £2,000. His only other income is employment income of £146,500 in the tax year 2021/22.

State Huang's taxable savings income for the tax year 2021/22.

Calculate Huang's income tax liability in respect of his savings income for the tax year 2021/22 to the nearest pound.

(b)   Rebecca owns two properties: 15 Olden Way and 29 Harrow Crescent. Both properties are let on a furnished basis and are rented out as follows:

1   15 Olden Way

The rent is £600 per month, payable on the 20th of the month, and the property was occupied throughout the whole of the tax year 2021/22. The rent payable in March was late, and not paid until 10 April 2022.

2   29 Harrow Crescent

The rent is £500 per month, payable on the first of the month. The property was occupied until 30 June 2021 when the tenants moved out. The new tenants moved in on 1 January 2022.

Rebecca elects to use the accruals basis.

(i)   **Calculate the rental income chargeable to income tax for Rebecca in the tax year 2021/22.**

Rebecca's expenses for the properties are:

	15 Olden Way £	29 Harrow Crescent £
Roof repair		1,500
Insurance:		
12 months to 31 December 2021 – paid 1 Jan 2021	150	120
12 months to 31 December 2022 – paid 1 Jan 2022	180	140
Total:		

(iii)   **Calculate Rebecca's allowable expenses in the tax year 2021/22.**

(c)   **Identify whether each of the following statements is true or false.**

Tick one box on each line.

	True	False
The property allowance is always automatically applied, although the taxpayer can elect not to claim it.		
Ben, a landlord, delays paying a March repair bill until 15 April 2022. He can deduct this bill from his property income for the tax year 2021/22 whether he uses the accruals basis or the cash basis.		

20   RAVI

(a)   In the tax year 2021/22 Ravi has trading profits of £22,000. The only other income he received during the year is the following investment income which was paid directly into his bank account:

Source of income	Amount
Interest from bank account	£2,450
Dividends from a stocks and shares ISA	£3,200
Dividends from Xi Plc	£14,000

Calculate the taxable dividends and the tax payable by Ravi on his dividend income and savings income, completing the table below. Show the tax payable in whole pounds.

	£
Taxable dividends	
Tax payable on dividend income	
Tax payable on savings income	

(b) Wilma owns a flat which she rents out for £3,600 per year. The property was unoccupied until 1 July 2021. Rent is paid monthly in advance.

On 1 May 2021 Wilma paid insurance of £300 in respect of the flat for the 12 months starting 1 May 2021.

(i) **Calculate the rental income chargeable to income tax for Wilma in the tax year 2021/22.**

[   ]

(ii) **Calculate Wilma's allowable expenses in the tax year 2021/22.**

[   ]

Redi bought a house, Long Close, on 1 August 2021. The property was unfurnished so Redi spent £3,000 furnishing the flat before tenants moved in on 1 November 2021. The monthly rental was £750 paid on the 1st of each month.

Redi paid insurance of £160 on 1 August 2021 for the year ended 31 July 2022. He incurred and paid water rates of £85 during the tax year 2021/22. He paid for repairs on the property of £900 in January 2022.

Redi has elected to use the accruals basis.

(i) **Calculate the rental income chargeable to income tax for Redi in the tax year 2021/22.**

[   ]

(ii) **Calculate Redi's allowable expenses in the tax year 2021/22.**

[   ]

(c) **Identify whether the following statements are true or false.**

Tick one box on each line.

	True	False
A taxpayer with gross rental income of more than £1,000 and expenses of less than £1,000 should always claim the property allowance		
Interest from NS&I Savings Certificates is exempt.		

21 HOWARD

(a) In the tax year 2021/22 Wilf received dividend income of £5,000. He has other income before the personal allowance of £45,000.

Calculate Wilf's income tax liability in respect of his dividend income in the tax year 2021/22 to the nearest pound.

[   ]

In the tax year 2021/22 Jamie received interest of £4,000 made up of interest on overpaid tax of £50 and £3,950 building society interest. He has other income of £130,000 in the tax year 2021/22.

State Jamie's taxable savings income for the tax year 2021/22.

Calculate Jamie's income tax liability in respect of his savings income for the tax year 2021/22 to the nearest pound.

(b) Howard drives 11,000 miles during the tax year 2021/22 in managing his property business. He incurs motor expenses of £6,100 in respect of this mileage, which was all paid during the tax year 2021/22.

Howard received monthly property income of £8,000 on 1st of each month, from a variety of properties. At 5 April 2022, amounts outstanding from tenants in relation to the tax year 2021/22 total £3,000. Howard had no outstanding amounts at the start of the year.

Calculate how much is deductible from his property income in respect of the above mileage in the tax year 2021/22.

Calculate the rental income chargeable to tax in the tax year 2021/22.

Rosalie rents out a number of properties and her gross rents for the year are £163,000. In respect of one of her houses, she paid insurance on 1 July 2020 of £1,800 for the year ended 30 June 2021 and £2,160 on the 1 July 2021 for the year ended 30 June 2022.

Calculate Rosalie's allowable expense against her property income in respect of this insurance.

(c) **Identify whether each of the following statements is true or false.**

Tick one box on each line.

	True	False
Losses made on renting out a property can only be offset against property profits.		
Any property losses which cannot be offset in the year they are incurred cannot be carried forward.		

INCOME TAX PAYABLE

22   FENFANG

During the tax year 2021/22 Fenfang received £70,000 salary (gross amount) and £40,200 of dividends (none from ISAs).

She paid a personal pension scheme contribution of £2,000 and made gift aid payments to charity totalling £160. PAYE of £15,500 was deducted from her salary.

Use the table below to calculate Fenfang's income tax payable for the tax year 2021/22. Show the income in whole pounds and the tax payable to the nearest pound.

23   MARYAM

During the tax year 2021/22 Maryam earned property income of £48,000. She also received interest from a bank account of £250, interest from an ISA of £300 and dividends of £14,000 from Xy Ltd.

Maryam has a property loss of £600 brought forward from the tax year 2020/21 and paid £40 per month in gift aid donations.

During the tax year 2021/22 Tommy earned a salary of £80,000 and paid 5% of this into his employer's occupational pension scheme. He also received building society interest of £3,000 and dividends of £1,000. PAYE of £17,000 was paid in the tax year 2021/22.

Use the table below to calculate Maryam's and Tommy's income tax payable for the tax year 2021/22. Show the income and tax payable in whole pounds.

24   LUCIA

During the tax year 2021/22 Lucia earned a salary of £40,000. She also received lottery winnings of £10,000, building society interest of £800 and dividends from Zi Ltd of £18,000.

Lucia paid 2% of her salary into her personal pension scheme during the year. She paid PAYE of £7,900 for the year.

Gareth made income from self-employment of £160,000 in the tax year 2021/22. He received building society interest of £580. He also received dividends of £30,000 of which £17,000 related to shares held in an ISA.

Use the table below to calculate Lucia's and Gareth's income tax payable for the tax year 2021/22. Show the income and the tax payable in whole pounds.

25 ROMAN

During the tax year 2021/22 Roman received a pension of £23,696, property income of £4,300, savings income of £2,720 and dividends of £6,144. He had a property loss brought forward from the tax year 2020/21 of £1,300.

During the tax year 2021/22 Alison made self-employment income of £113,000. She made a monthly payment to her personal pension scheme of £800. In January 2022 she gave a cash donation of £1,000 to a registered charity and claimed gift aid.

Use the table below to calculate Roman's and Alison's income tax liability for the tax year 2021/22. Show the income in whole pounds and the tax liability to the nearest pound.

26 RAY

During the tax year 2021/22 Ray had employment income of £120,870 before he contributed £10,000 into his employer's occupation pension scheme and his employer contributed £8,000.

In the tax year 2021/22 Ray received savings income of £3,900 of which £200 relates to savings in an ISA. Ray made a gift aid payment of £400 in May 2021 and paid PAYE of £34,000 in the tax year 2021/22.

Use the table below to calculate Ray's income tax payable for the tax year 2021/22. Show the answer in whole pounds.

27 JJ

During the tax year 2021/22 JJ received employment income of £148,200, building society interest of £7,150 and dividends of £7,556.

JJ made cash donations to charity of £100 each month. He claimed gift aid on the donations.

JJ's PAYE deductions for the tax year 2021/22 were £51,800.

Use the table below to calculate JJ's income tax payable for the tax year 2021/22. Show the income in whole pounds and the tax liability to the nearest pound.

28   BILL

During the tax year 2021/22 Bill had employment income of £54,600 (PAYE deducted of £9,340) and received building society interest of £3,000.

During the tax year 2021/22 Erica had property income of £140,000. She received dividends of £15,000 of which £6,000 was received from shares held in an ISA. She had losses brought forward from her property business of £10,000 and made a payment into her personal pension scheme of £8,000 in March 2022.

Use the table below to calculate Bill's and Erica's income tax payable/repayable for the tax year 2021/22. Show your answer in whole pounds.

NATIONAL INSURANCE CONTRIBUTIONS

29   JEREMY

(a)   Jeremy received the following from his employer Hawk Ltd in the tax year 2021/22.

	£
Salary	31,000
Taxable benefit	800

Jeremy made pension contributions of £2,400 in 2021/22.

Hawk Ltd also employs Aishah, she received a salary of £9,510 and taxable benefits of £7,200.

Complete the following calculations. Answer in whole pounds. Enter 0 (zero) if the answer is nil. Ignore the employment allowance.

Calculate the class 1 national insurance contributions payable by Jeremy for the tax year 2021/22.

Calculate the class 1 national insurance contributions payable by Aishah for the tax year 2021/22.

Calculate the total employer class 1 national insurance contributions payable by Hawk Ltd in the tax year 2021/22 in respect of Jeremy and Aishah.

Calculate the class 1A national insurance contributions payable by Hawk Ltd in the tax year 2021/22 in respect of Jeremy and Aishah.

(b)   **Identify whether the following statement is true or false in connection with class 1 national insurance contributions.**

Tick the appropriate box for each statement.

	True	False
Bo is a self-employed entertainer at children's parties making a profit of £35,000 per year. Bo is required to pay class 1 employee contributions in respect of this profit.		

30 MURRAY

(a) Lob Roll Ltd employs two employees, Joan and Murray.

Joan received a salary of £20,000 and no benefits in the tax year 2021/22. In the tax year 2021/22 Murray received the following:

	£
Salary	126,000
Taxable benefit	14,400

Murray made pension contributions of £27,000 in the tax year 2021/22. He also incurred expenses of £4,650 wholly, exclusively and necessarily in the performance of his duties.

Your answers to this question should all be in pounds and pence.

Calculate Joan's liability to class 1 national insurance contributions for the tax year 2021/22.

Calculate Murray's liability to class 1 national insurance contributions for the tax year 2021/22.

Calculate Lob Roll Ltd's liability to employer class 1 national insurance contributions for the tax year 2021/22.

Calculate Lob Roll Ltd's liability to class 1A national insurance contributions for the tax year 2021/22.

(b) **Identify whether the following statement is true or false in connection with class 1 national insurance contributions.**

Tick the appropriate box for each statement.

	True	False
Ting has two jobs, one job pays £4,000 per year and the other one pays £9,000. Ting is required to pay class 1 employee contributions.		

31 LUKA

(a) Luka is employed by Hounds Ltd. In the tax year 2021/22 Luka received a gross salary of £4,800 per month. He also received taxable benefits totalling £8,300. None of the benefits is convertible into cash.

Noel is also employed by Hounds Ltd. He received a salary of £4,000 per month throughout the tax year 2021/22 and no taxable benefits.

Your answers to this question should all be in whole pounds. Ignore the employment allowance.

Calculate Luka's liability to class 1 national insurance contributions for the tax year 2021/22.

[   ]

Calculate Noel's liability to class 1 national insurance contributions for the tax year 2021/22.

[   ]

Calculate Hounds Ltd's liability to employer class 1 national insurance contributions for the tax year 2021/22 in respect of Luka and Noel.

[   ]

Calculate Hounds Ltd's liability to class 1A national insurance contributions for the tax year 2021/22 in respect of Luka and Noel.

[   ]

(b)   Advise whether the following statement is true or false in connection with class 1 national insurance contributions.

Tick the appropriate box.

	True	False
In the tax year 2021/22 Michael earned a gross salary of £37,000. He contributed £3,800 to an occupational pension scheme during the year. Michael's total liability to national insurance contributions for the tax year 2021/22 is £3,291.84 ((£37,000 – £9,568) × 12%).		

32   LEWIS

(a)   Lewis is employed as a director by Auto Ltd. In the tax year 2021/22 Lewis received the following from his employer:

	£
Salary	71,000
Bonus	11,000

Janine also works for Auto Ltd earning an annual salary of £25,000.

Your answers to this question should all be in pounds and pence, and calculated on an annual basis. Ignore the employment allowance.

Calculate Lewis' liability to class 1 national insurance contributions for the tax year 2021/22.

[   ]

Calculate Janine's liability to class 1 national insurance contributions for the tax year 2021/22.

[   ]

Calculate Auto Ltd's liability to class 1 national insurance contributions for the tax year 2021/22 in respect of Lewis and Janine.

[   ]

(b) Select whether each of the following statements is true or false in connection with class 1 national insurance contributions.

Tick the appropriate box for each statement.

	True	False
In the tax year 2021/22 Amber earned a salary of £40,000. She was also provided with a company car resulting in a taxable benefit of £3,700. Amber's total liability to national insurance contributions for 2021/22 is £4,095.84 ((£40,000 + £3,700 – £9,568) × 12%).		
John has a salary of £30,000 and pays 5% of his salary into an occupational pension scheme. John's employer will pay class 1 national insurance contributions on £30,000.		

33 NAOMIE

(a) Naomie is employed by Pirates Ltd. In the tax year 2021/22 Naomie received a gross salary of £39,000. She was also provided with a company car resulting in a taxable benefit of £2,150.

Jeff is the only other employee of Pirates Ltd. In the tax year 2021/22 he received a gross salary of £110,000 and had taxable benefits of £2,000.

Your answers to this question should all be in whole pounds.

Calculate Naomie's liability to class 1 national insurance contributions for the tax year 2021/22.

[   ]

Calculate Jeff's liability to class 1 national insurance contributions for the tax year 2021/22.

[   ]

Calculate Pirates Ltd's liability to class 1 national insurance contributions for the tax year 2021/22.

[   ]

Calculate Pirates Ltd's liability to class 1A national insurance contributions for the tax year 2021/22.

[   ]

(b) Select whether the following statement is true or false in connection with class 1 national insurance contributions.

Tick the appropriate box.

	True	False
Phillip has a salary of £9,400. He is paid 60p a mile for 6,000 business miles. Phillip has no national insurance liability in the tax year 2021/22.		

34   REG

(a)   Reg and Lisa are both employed by Lleaff Ltd and in the tax year 2021/22 Reg received a salary of £160,000 and Lisa received a salary of £50,000.

Your answers to this question should all be in pounds and pence. Ignore the employment allowance.

Calculate Reg' liability to class 1 national insurance contributions for the tax year 2021/22.

```
┌─────────────────────────┐
│                         │
└─────────────────────────┘
```

Calculate Lisa's liability to class 1 national insurance contributions for the tax year 2021/22.

```
┌─────────────────────────┐
│                         │
└─────────────────────────┘
```

Calculate Lleaff Ltd's liability to class 1 national insurance contributions for the tax year 2021/22 in respect of Reg and Lisa.

```
┌─────────────────────────┐
│                         │
└─────────────────────────┘
```

(b)   **Select whether each of the following statements is true or false in connection with national insurance contributions.**

Tick the appropriate box for each statement.

	True	False
An employer only qualifies for the employment allowance if its class 1 and class 1A national insurance liabilities were less than £100,000 in the previous year.		
Contributions by an employee to the employer's occupation pension scheme are deducted from salary when calculating class 1 national insurance contributions.		

35   SALLY

(a)   Sally and Lance are employed by Twigg Ltd. In the tax year 2021/22 Sally received a gross salary of £36,000. She made a pension contribution to Twigg Ltd's occupational pension scheme of £1,000 in the tax year 2021/22.

Lance received a salary of £84,000 in the tax year 2021/22.

Your answers to this question should all be in whole pounds. Ignore the employment allowance.

Calculate Sally's liability to class 1 national insurance contributions for the tax year 2021/22.

```
┌─────────────────────────┐
│                         │
└─────────────────────────┘
```

Calculate Lance's liability to class 1 national insurance contributions for the tax year 2021/22.

```
┌─────────────────────────┐
│                         │
└─────────────────────────┘
```

Calculate Twigg Ltd's liability to employer class 1 national insurance contributions for the tax year 2021/22 in respect of Sally and Lance.

```
┌─────────────────────────┐
│                         │
└─────────────────────────┘
```

(b) Select whether each of the following statements is true or false in connection with national insurance contributions.

Tick the appropriate box for each statement.

	True	False
The employment allowance is not available if there is only one employee and the employee is a director.		
An employee pays class 1A national insurance contributions on their taxable benefits.		

TAX PLANNING

36 FREYA

(a) Freya is to be provided with a petrol driven company car on 6 April 2021 (the car will be registered on this date). The car will have CO_2 emissions of 108g/km and a list price of £17,400.

Freya's employer will pay for the petrol used by Freya for business purposes, of £2,800 per year, and for private purposes, of £1,700 per year.

Freya is a higher rate taxpayer.

Enter your answers in whole pounds. Enter 0 (zero) if the answer is nil.

(i) Calculate how much income tax Freya will save annually if she contributes £2,000 towards the capital cost of the car.	£
(ii) Calculate how much income tax Freya will save annually if she contributes £600 per year towards the cost of using the car for private purposes.	£
(iii) Calculate how much income tax Freya will save annually if she contributes £480 per year towards the cost of the private use petrol.	£

(b) Richard earns a salary of £45,000 and has no other income in the tax year 2021/22. He wants to know the reduction in his income tax liability for the tax year 2021/22 if he donates cash of £200 to a registered charity and claims gift aid.

Calculate the reduction in Richard's income tax liability if Richard makes the charitable donation. Enter your answer in whole pounds. Enter 0 (zero) if the answer is nil.

37 CHRISTINA

(a) Christina's employer pays 45p per mile for Christina to use her own car for business miles. Alternatively, the company pays for Christina's ticket if she travels by train for business purposes.

In the tax year 2021/22 Christina used her car for 10,800 business miles. This included 500 miles to attend a London conference. A train ticket to the conference would have cost £350.

Christina is a higher rate taxpayer.

Calculate Christina's income tax saving if she had taken the train to London rather than driving. Enter your answer in whole pounds. Enter 0 (zero) if the answer is nil.

```
┌────────────────────────┐
│                        │
└────────────────────────┘
```

(b) Russell, a higher rate taxpayer, is provided with a house by his employer during the tax year 2021/22. This is not job-related accommodation. The house cost his employer £160,000 in March 2021, when it was first provided to Russell.

The employer also owns a flat bought for £70,000 in January 2002. The market value in March 2021 is £140,000.

Russell wants to know how much tax he could have saved if he had moved into flat in March 2021 rather than the house. Assume the flat and the house have the same annual values.

Calculate Russell's income tax saving for the tax year 2021/22 if he had lived in the flat. Enter your answer in whole pounds. Enter 0 (zero) if the answer is nil.

```
┌────────────────────────┐
│                        │
└────────────────────────┘
```

(c) Bogdan received a salary of £40,000 in the tax year 2021/22. He received dividends of £7,000 on shares he bought during the year. He realises he should have invested the money to buy the shares in an individual savings account and wants to know how much tax this would have saved.

Calculate Bogdan's income tax saving if the shares were instead held in an individual savings account giving the same dividends. Enter your answer in whole pounds. Enter 0 (zero) if the answer is nil.

```
┌────────────────────────┐
│                        │
└────────────────────────┘
```

(d) Diane has employment income of £60,000 and building society interest of £1,000 in the tax year 2021/22. She already makes contributions to her personal pension scheme of £500 per month.

Diane's daughter has told her that if she were a basic rate taxpayer she would be able to benefit from the £1,000 savings allowance and pay no tax on the building society interest. Diana wants to know what further single payment she should make into her personal pension scheme so that she becomes a basic rate taxpayer.

Calculate the minimum further payment Diane should make to her pension scheme to pay no tax on the interest. Enter your answer in whole pounds. Enter 0 (zero) if the answer is nil.

```
┌────────────────────────┐
│                        │
└────────────────────────┘
```

38   **MITCHELL**

(a)   Mitchell is provided with a diesel driven company car from 1 February 2021. The car was registered on 1 January 2020. The car has CO_2 emissions of 116g/km, a list price of £22,300 and does not meet the RDE2 standards.

Mitchell contributes £6,000 towards the capital cost of the car.

Identify how the following changes to Mitchell's benefit will affect the income tax charge for the tax year 2021/22. Assume each change is the only adjustment to the information above.

	Increase	Decrease	No change
Mitchell contributes a further £1,500 towards the capital cost of the car.			
Mitchell has £185 of accessories added to the car on 6 April 2021.			
A car is provided to the same specification but registered on 1 January 2021.			
A car is provided to the same specification but the RDE2 standards are met.			

(b)   Sandra had a salary of £150,000 and bank interest of £500 in the tax year 2021/22. She wants to know how much income tax she could have saved if she had made a contribution to her employer's occupational pension scheme of £500.

Calculate the saving in income tax due on the salary if Sandra had made the pension contribution. Enter your answer in whole pounds. Enter 0 (zero) if the answer is nil.

Calculate the saving in income tax due on the bank interest if Sandra had made the pension contribution. Enter your answer in whole pounds. Enter zero (0) if the answer is nil.

39   **MADELINE**

(a)   Madeline's employer pays a flat rate per mile for use of employees' own cars for business purposes. Madeline travelled 20,000 business miles using her own car in 2021/22.

Calculate the maximum rate per mile for the payments made by the employer such that Madeline pays no income tax on the mileage payments. Enter your answer in whole pence.

(b) Tanya has a salary of £103,000 in 2021/22. Her employer also pays her annual subscription at a members' gym of £1,000. Tanya has no other taxable income.

Tanya's employer has decided to offer gym facilities at its offices for employees only. The cost of running the gym will be £420 per employee per annum. Tanya hopes using this instead of the gym membership will save her tax.

Enter your answers in whole pounds. Enter 0 (zero) if the answer is nil.

The decrease in Tanya's employment income in 2021/22 if her employer had provided the work gym, rather than paid for her gym membership would be

```

```

The increase in Tanya's personal allowance in the tax year 2021/22 if her employer had provided the work gym, rather than paid for her gym membership would be

```

```

(c) Lexi, an additional rate taxpayer, had use of a company car throughout the tax year 2021/22. The petrol car had CO_2 emissions of 121g/km and was first registered in August 2020. Lexi's taxable car benefit for the tax year 2021/22 was £8,960.

Lexi is keen to use a hybrid car instead, with the same list price but CO_2 emissions of 35g/km and an electric range of 50 miles. She wants to know how much tax she could have saved using the hybrid.

Calculate Lexi's income tax saving if her employer had provided the hybrid car throughout the tax year 2021/22 rather than the petrol car. Enter your answer in whole pounds. Enter 0 (zero) if the answer is nil.

```

```

(d) Tariq is an additional rate taxpayer with employment and interest income. The interest income is derived from an investment of £10,000 made into an individual savings account in 2020/21.

Tariq has £100,000 to invest in shares in 2021/22 and will make the maximum investment for this purpose in an individual savings account in 2021/22. He wants to know his income tax liability on dividends if the entire investment yields a 5% dividend in 2021/22.

Calculate Tariq's income tax on his dividends in 2021/22. Enter your answer in whole pounds. Enter zero (0) if the answer is nil.

```

```

40 ANITA

(a) Anita works for a catering company and is provided for van to make deliveries to customers. Anita also uses the van to get to work each day and for transporting sports equipment for the football club she coaches in her spare time.

The van is a diesel van with CO_2 emissions of 151g/km and was first registered in April 2018. It does not meet the RDE2 standards. The company pays for diesel for the deliveries only.

Identify how the following changes to Anita's benefit will affect the income tax charge for the tax year 2021/22. Assume each change is the only adjustment to the information above.

Proposed change	Increase	Decrease	No change
Anita stops using the van personally except for travel to work.			
Anita makes a £50 per month contribution towards private use of the van.			
Anita made a capital contribution of £2,000 towards the purchase of the van.			
The van is changed for a zero emissions model.			
The van is changed for a model with CO_2 emissions of 189g/km.			
The company pays for all fuel used by the van.			

(b) Frank received dividends of £160,000 and had no other income in the tax year 2021/22. He wants to know how much income tax he could have saved if he had made a cash donation of £8,000 to a registered charity under gift aid.

Calculate Frank's income tax saving if he had made the donation. Enter your answer in whole pounds. Enter 0 (zero) if the answer is nil.

```
[                    ]
```

41   TIM

(a) As part of Tim's employment he stays away from home, working elsewhere in the UK. He drives his own car, receiving the approved mileage allowance for business miles.

Two other employees travel with Tim. His employer gives Tim an allowance for driving these employees.

Tim receives an allowance of £12 for each night he is away which covers incidental expenses such as hotel laundry.

Tim is concerned about the tax implications of the allowances for travel with the other employees and for daily incidental expenses.

State the total allowance per mile Tim could receive, without paying tax, in respect of the two employees. Enter your answer in pence.

```
[                    ]
```

State the amount by which the daily incidental allowance should decrease so that Tim pays no income tax on this. Enter your answer in whole pounds.

```
[                    ]
```

(b) Ian's employer has given Ian private use of a TV since 6 April 2020. The TV cost the employer £2,000 in March 2020. Ian did not pay his employer for use of the TV.

On 6 April 2021 Ian's employer gave him the TV outright. The market value of the TV at that date was £1,300. Ian made a contribution for the TV such that no income tax arises on the gift.

Calculate the minimum amount Ian had to pay for the TV to suffer no income tax on the gift. Enter your answers in whole pounds. Enter 0 (zero) if the answer is nil.

```
┌─────────────────────────┐
│                         │
└─────────────────────────┘
```

(c) Yogi has employment income of £160,000 in 2021/22. He inherited £20,000 from his mother and invested £10,000 in a building society account giving him 2% interest in 2021/22. Yogi invested the remaining £10,000 in shares which gave him a 7% dividend in 2021/22.

He realises that he could have invested the funds via individual savings accounts (ISAs).

Calculate Yogi's income tax saving in 2021/22 if ISAs had been used to invest in the same proportion of cash and shares, with the same returns before tax. Enter your answer in whole pounds. Enter 0 (zero) if the answer is nil.

```
┌─────────────────────────┐
│                         │
└─────────────────────────┘
```

(d) Aoife earns a salary of £105,000. Her employer held a winter party in December 2021 which cost the company £400 per employee.

Aoife received building society interest of £200 in 2021/22.

Aoife wants to make a payment to a registered charity, on which she will claim gift aid, sufficient to preserve her personal allowance for 2021/22.

Calculate the minimum payment Aoife should make to the charity. Enter your answer in whole pounds. Enter 0 (zero) if the answer is nil.

```
┌─────────────────────────┐
│                         │
└─────────────────────────┘
```

42 PHILIP

(a) In 2021/22 Philip received a salary of £60,000. He was also provided with an expensive house to live in by his employer for which the taxable benefit was £12,000.

Philip's employer contributes 5% of basic salary into Philip's personal pension scheme. Philip contributes 8%.

Philip inherited cash of 20,000 in May 2021 and invested this in an individual savings account giving interest of £200 in 2021/22.

Identify how the following changes would affect Philip's income tax liability for the tax year 2021/22. Assume each change is the only adjustment to the information above.

Proposed change	Increase	Decrease	No change
Philip decreases his contribution to his personal pension scheme.			
An extension is built to the house in May 2021.			
Philip pays rent of £100 per week to live in the house.			
Philip had instead invested the £20,000 cash in a five-year building society account (not an individual savings account) on which he received interest of £1,000 in 2021/22.			

(b) Roger is starting work for a new employer. His employer will pay £10,000 to help Roger move house closer to the company. The company will also give Roger a loan of £20,000 to buy a car for business and private use. The interest rate on the loan will be 1.25% per annum.

State the amount by which the relocation payment should be reduced for Roger to avoid paying income tax on this payment. Enter your answer in whole pounds. Enter 0 (zero) if the answer is nil.

```
[                    ]
```

Calculate the increase in the amount of annual interest Roger should pay to avoid paying income tax on the loan. Enter your answer in whole pounds. Enter 0 (zero) if the answer is nil.

```
[                    ]
```

Roger is an additional rate taxpayer. He commits to paying 1% of his salary to charity each month. He claims gift aid on the payment made. His annual salary in 2021/22 is £230,000.

Calculate Roger's income tax saving on his charitable donations for 2021/22. Enter your answer in whole pounds. Enter 0 (zero) if the answer is nil.

```
[                    ]
```

CAPITAL GAINS TAX PRINCIPLES

43   TAREQ

(a)   For each statement, tick the appropriate box.

	Actual proceeds used	Deemed proceeds used	No gain/ no loss basis
Sister gives an asset to her brother			
Civil partner gives an asset to civil partner			
Tareq sells an asset to his friend for £38,000. He later discovers the asset is worth £45,000.			

(b)   Reyansh has disposed of the non-wasting chattels below.

For each of the following asset disposals, select whether there is a gain, a loss or whether the disposal is exempt. Enter the amount of the gain or loss, as a positive figure, in the final column. Enter 0 (zero) if there is no gain or loss.

Asset	Sale proceeds	Cost	Select one option	£
1	£5,000	£4,000	gain/loss/exempt	
2	£10,000	£7,000	gain/loss/exempt	
3	£9,000	£3,000	gain/loss/exempt	
4	£4,000	£9,000	gain/loss/exempt	

(c)   Beatriz bought an antique set of 6 chairs in August 2017 for £15,000, and then sold two of them in January 2022 for £10,000. The market value of the remaining 4 chairs is £25,000.

Calculate the allowable cost of the chairs in the chargeable gain calculation.

44   SAMANTHA

(a)   **For each statement, tick the appropriate box.**

	Actual proceeds used	Deemed proceeds used	No gain no loss basis
Samantha sells an asset to her colleague for £8,000. She then discovers that it was worth £10,000.			
Neil sells an asset to his wife for £10,000 when the market value is £14,000			
Selim gives an asset to his friend.			

(b) **For each of the following disposals select whether the disposal gives rise to a gain, a loss, or is exempt and give the amount of the gain or loss. Enter the amount as a positive number. Enter 0 (zero) for an exempt amount.**

	Select one option	£
A racehorse bought for £4,000 and sold for £7,500	gain/loss/exempt	
A necklace bought for £5,900 plus £200 of auction costs, and given away when its market value was £8,000	gain/loss/exempt	
An antique vase bought for £3,000 and sold for £8,200	gain/loss/exempt	
A painting bought for £3,000 and sold for £5,900	gain/loss/amount	

(c) Harry bought a second property as an investment in February 2015 for £155,000. He built a conservatory costing £15,000 and an extension which cost £28,000 during 2016. In 2017 he redecorated the property at a cost of £2,200.

In March 2022 he sold the entire property for £400,000.

Calculate the gain on disposal of this asset.

45 VICTORIA

(a) **Identify whether each of the following statements is true or false.**

Tick ONE box in each row.

	True	False
Victoria and her cousin Olive are connected persons for capital gains purposes.		
A gift from Janet to her husband Mike cannot give rise to a gain or a loss.		
If an asset is destroyed by flooding and insurance proceeds are received this is a chargeable disposal.		

(b) Individuals made the following disposals to unconnected persons during the tax year 2021/22.

Calculate the chargeable gain for each disposal. Enter your answer in whole pounds. Enter 0 (zero) if the answer is nil.

	Gain £
Jay bought a building for £70,000. He spent £10,000 on repairs to the building and sold it for £120,000.	
Carli bought an asset for £30,000, selling it for £50,000. She paid auctioneer's commission of 5% when she bought the asset and 4% when she sold the asset.	
Kamilah died on 3 October 2021. She left an antique desk to charity in her will. The desk had cost her £13,000 and was valued for probate at £27,000.	
Rory owned a set of three paintings. He had bought these for £16,500 in total. He sold one of the paintings for £20,000. The remaining two paintings had a total market value of £36,000.	
James bought a vintage car for £11,500 and sold it for £15,000.	

46   ESHE

(a) Identify whether the following statements about disposals of assets are true or false.

Tick ONE box in each row.

	True	False
A chargeable gain arises on the gift to a connected person of a necklace costing £8,000 which has increased in value.		
No gain or loss arises if insurance proceeds are received for a painting destroyed in a fire.		
A sale to a friend at an intended discount uses the market value for deemed proceeds in the gains calculation.		

(b) Eshe and Alvin are unconnected persons. They made the following disposals during the tax year 2021/22.

Calculate the chargeable gain for each disposal. Enter your answer in whole pounds. Enter 0 (zero) if the answer is nil.

	Gain £
Eshe	
Eshe sold a necklace worth £50,000 to her sister for £40,000. The necklace had cost Eshe £31,400 in June 2009.	
Eshe gave a painting to her wife's brother. The painting cost £5,700 and was worth £9,000 at the time of the gift.	
Eshe sold an antique table which had cost £8,000 to her cousin for £11,000. This was the price that an antique dealer had offered to Eshe earlier in the year. Later Eshe discovered its value was in fact £12,000.	
Alvin	
Alvin bought a 10 acre field in May 2010 for £40,000. In June 2021 he sold 4 acres for £83,000 net of £2,000 selling expenses. The remaining 6 acres were valued at £110,000.	
In December 2021 Alvin sold the remaining 6 acres of land for £118,000 which was the gross proceeds before incurring £1,500 selling expenses.	

47 SAUL

(a) Identify whether each of the following is chargeable or exempt for capital gains tax purposes.

Tick ONE box in each row.

	Chargeable	Exempt
A machine used in a business and valued at £10,000		
An individual aged under 18 years old		
A gift of a painting (worth £50,000) to a charity		

(b) Saul has disposed of the non-wasting chattels below.

For each of the following asset disposals, select whether there is a gain, a loss or whether the disposal is exempt. Enter the amount of the gain or loss, as a positive figure, in the final column. Enter 0 (zero) if there is no gain or loss.

Asset	Sale proceeds	Cost	Select one option	£
1	£5,000	£6,000	gain/loss/exempt	
2	£8,000	£4,000	gain/loss/exempt	
3	£7,000	£6,500	gain/loss/exempt	
4	£5,000	£7,000	gain/loss/exempt	

(c)   Joaquin bought an asset for £180,000. He spent £10,000 on repairs and £60,000 on improvements. He sold the asset for £300,000.

Calculate the gain on the sale of the asset.

[   ]

48   **MARTOK**

(a)   **Identify whether each of the following is chargeable or exempt for capital gains tax purposes.**

Tick ONE box in each row.

	Chargeable	Exempt
An antique clock valued at £20,000		
An individual who has no taxable income		
The sale of part of a plot of land		

(b)   Martok has disposed of the following assets in the tax year 2021/22.

For each of the following asset disposals, select whether there is a gain, a loss or whether the disposal is exempt. Enter the amount of the gain or loss, as a positive figure, in the final column. Enter 0 (zero) if there is no gain or loss.

	Select one option	£
A bravery medal Martok inherited from his father, who had been awarded the medal. The medal was worth £6,400 when Martok inherited it. He sold it for £8,000.	gain/loss/exempt	
A painting which Martok had bought for £13,000 and sold for £4,000.	gain/loss/exempt	
Antique violin sold for £150,000. Martok incurred auctioneer's fees of 1% on this amount. The violin had cost £120,000.	gain/loss/exempt	
A ring inherited from his mother which she had bought for £2,000. Its value on inheritance was £8,000 and it was sold for £14,000.	gain/loss/exempt	
Shares held in an ISA bought for £5,000 and sold for £35,000.	gain/loss/exempt	

(c)   Sara sold five acres of land in December 2021 for £68,600 after deduction of solicitor's fees of 2% of the gross proceeds. The five acres were part of a total plot of eight acres which Sara had bought for £80,000 in June 2012. In December 2021 the remaining three acres were worth £40,000.

Calculate the gain on disposal of the five acres of land. Enter your answer in whole pounds.

[   ]

49 BARNEY

(a) **Identify whether the following statements about disposals of assets are true or false.**

Tick ONE box in each row.

	True	False
The death of a taxpayer does not give rise to chargeable disposals.		
Market value is used for the proceeds on disposal of a chargeable asset between civil partners.		
A brother and a sister are connected persons for capital gains tax purposes.		

(b) Barney made the following disposals during the tax year 2021/22.

Calculate the chargeable gain for each disposal. Enter your answer in whole pounds. Enter 0 (zero) if the answer is nil.

	Gain £
Barney gave his daughter cash of £25,000.	
A statue owned by Barney was destroyed in a storm. Barney received insurance proceeds of £50,000. He had bought the statue for £23,000 in January 2003.	
Barney sold antique furniture to his son for £20,000. The market value was £25,000 but Barney thought the sale to his son was easier than advertising this online. The furniture had cost Barney £19,000 in 2012 and he had paid £500 for expert polishing of the furniture in 2015.	
Barney sold a vase for £3,200 which had cost £2,000.	
Barney sold the remaining two acres of a plot of land for £100,000. He had bought five acres for £40,000 in 2003 but sold three acres in 2017 for £90,000. At the time of the 2017 sale, the remaining two acres were worth £50,000.	

CAPITAL GAINS TAX: DISPOSALS OF SHARES

50 STRINGER LTD

John holds shares in Stringer Ltd. His transactions in Stringer Ltd shares are as shown in the table.

Date	Transaction information
1 July 2012	Purchase of 8,000 shares for £8 per share
1 March 2013	Purchase of 4,000 shares for £9 per share
29 July 2015	Sale of 3,000 shares for £20,000
5 May 2019	1 for 1 bonus issue
10 February 2022	Sale of 5,000 shares for £10 per share

Clearly showing the balance of shares, and their value to carry forward, calculate the gain made on the shares sold in February 2022.

All workings must be shown in your calculations.

51 LULU LTD

Habiba holds shares in Lulu Ltd. Her transactions in Lulu Ltd shares are as shown in the table.

Date	Transaction information
3 October 2010	Purchase of 6,000 shares for £3 per share
14 May 2011	Purchase of 6,000 shares for £5 per share
5 June 2012	1 for 12 bonus issue
12 April 2016	Sale of 3,000 shares for £5 per share
30 January 2022	Sale of 8,000 shares for £7 per share

Clearly showing the balance of shares, and their value to carry forward, calculate the gain made on the shares sold in January 2022.

All workings must be shown in your calculations.

52   GILBERT LTD

Yasmine holds shares in Gilbert Ltd. Her transactions in Gilbert Ltd shares are as shown in the table.

Date	Transaction information
10 May 2009	Purchase of 8,000 shares for £6 per share
3 June 2013	1 for 2 bonus issue
7 September 2021	Sale of 8,000 shares for £65,000
15 September 2021	Purchase of 1,200 shares for £9,600
18 September 2021	Purchase of 1,000 shares for £10,000

Clearly showing the balance of shares, and their value, to carry forward calculate the gain made on these shares.

All workings must be shown in your calculations.

53 BELLA

Bella holds shares in Nessie Ltd. Her transactions in Nessie Ltd shares are as shown in the table.

Date	Transaction information
9 September 2012	Purchase of 20,000 shares for £6 per share
10 July 2014	Sale of 4,000 shares for £7 per share
14 June 2016	Take up of 1 for 8 rights issue at £4 per share
14 May 2021	Sale of 9,000 shares for £11 per share
17 May 2021	Purchase of 1,000 shares for £10 per share

Clearly showing the balance of shares, and their value, to carry forward calculate the gain made on these shares.

All workings must be shown in your calculations.

54 BAJOR PLC

Mohamed has the following transactions in the shares of Bajor plc:

		Number of shares	Cost/proceeds
February 2010	Purchased	2,000	£7,560
July 2012	Bonus issue	1 for 10	
December 2014	Purchased	500	£2,800
April 2016	Rights issue	1 for 5	£2.50 per share
March 2022	Sold	2,500	£17,500

Clearly showing the balance of shares, and their value, to carry forward calculate the gain or loss made on these shares.

All workings must be shown in your calculations.

55 ASPEN LTD

Kerry holds shares in Aspen Ltd. Her transactions in Aspen Ltd shares are as shown in the table.

Date	Transaction information
10 November 2016	Purchase of 4,000 shares for £5 per share
1 July 2018	1 for 2 bonus issue
18 June 2021	Sale of 2,000 shares for £6 per share
18 June 2021	Purchase of 200 shares for £5.50 per share
25 June 2021	Purchase of 400 shares for £7 per share

Clearly showing the balance of shares, and their value, to carry forward calculate the gain made on these shares.

All workings must be shown in your calculations.

56 CHERY LTD

Fred holds shares in Chery Ltd. His transactions in Chery Ltd shares are as shown in the table.

Date	Transaction information
15 August 2013	Purchase of 10,000 shares for £8 per share
2 September 2015	Take up 1 for 2 rights issue at £6 per share
18 February 2019	Sale of 3,000 shares for £10 per share
19 January 2022	Purchase of 2,000 shares for £12 per share
31 January 2022	Sale of 7,000 shares for £91,000

Clearly showing the balance of shares, and their value, to carry forward calculate the gain made on these shares.

All workings must be shown in your calculations.

CAPITAL GAINS TAX: RELIEFS AND EXEMPTIONS

57 JOANNA

(a) **Advise Joanna whether the following statements are true or false.**

Tick the appropriate box for each statement.

	True	False
Capital gains are taxed at 10% for all taxpayers.		
If a taxpayer does not use their annual exempt amount in the tax year 2020/21 they can bring it forward to use in the tax year 2021/22.		
The use of brought forward losses is made after the annual exempt amount.		
The last nine months of ownership of a main residence are treated as a period of occupation for private residence relief.		

(b) Paul made the following gains and losses in recent years:

Year	2019/20	2020/21	2021/22
Annual exempt amount £	12,000	12,300	12,300
Gains £	15,000	24,960	28,940
Loss £	4,180	1,400	2,130

Calculate Paul's taxable gains for the tax year 2021/22. Enter 0 (zero) if the answer is nil.

```

```

Calculate Paul's allowable losses carried forward to the tax year 2022/23. Enter 0 (zero) if the answer is nil.

```

```

(c) Agustin has an annual salary of £47,000 for the tax year 2021/22 and no other income.

He sold a painting in December 2021 for £25,927 which he originally purchased for £8,000 in August 2013. He paid 2% commission on the sale. This was his only capital disposal in 2021/22.

Calculate Agustin's taxable gains for the tax year 2021/22.

```

```

Calculate Agustin's capital gains tax payable for the tax year 2021/22 to the nearest pound.

```

```

58   **KEVIN**

(a)   **Kevin has made the following statements. Advise Kevin whether they are true or false.**

Tick the appropriate box for each statement.

	True	False
Unused personal allowance can be deducted from taxable gains.		
A taxpayer can live away from their main residence for any reason for up to five years and benefit from full private residence relief.		
Current year capital losses are restricted to protect the annual exempt amount.		
A capital loss made on a disposal to a connected person can only be deducted from gains on disposals to the same connected person.		

(b)   Esme bought a house on 1 July 2011 for £40,000.

She lived in the house until 30 June 2013 when she left to travel the world for a year.

She then moved back in until 30 June 2016 when she left to move in with her boyfriend.

The house remained unoccupied until she sold it on 30 June 2021 for £285,000.

This house is Esme's only property.

The chargeable gain on the sale of the house is   £

(c)   Ruth made the following gains and losses in recent years:

Year	Losses £	Gain £	Annual exempt amount £
2019/20	15,690	9,340	12,000
2020/21	1,500	16,700	12,300
2021/22	25,670	46,900	12,300

Calculate Ruth's taxable gains for the tax year 2021/22. Enter 0 (zero) if the answer is nil.

Calculate Ruth's allowable losses carried forward to the tax year 2022/23. Enter 0 (zero) if the answer is nil.

(d)   Arlene has a chargeable gain of £31,900 in respect of the disposal of an office held for investment purposes and £4,100 of capital losses for the tax year 2021/22. She has £7,200 of her basic rate band unused.

Calculate Arlene's capital gains tax payable for the tax year 2021/22 to the nearest pound.

59 ANGELA

(a) **Select whether each of the following statements is true or false.**

Tick the appropriate box for each statement.

	True	False
Unused annual exempt amount can be transferred to a spouse or civil partner.		
Unused allowable losses are carried forward to be deducted from chargeable gains in future tax years.		
Taxpayers can have several main residences for private residence relief provided they live at least nine months in each one.		
Capital gains tax is paid at 20% on gains made by a higher rate taxpayer.		

(b) Mo made the following gains and losses in recent years:

Year	Gains £	Losses £	Annual exempt amount £
2019/20	25,800	14,600	12,000
2020/21	8,900	23,500	12,300
2021/22	6,300	0	12,300

Calculate the amount chargeable to capital gains tax for the tax year 2021/22. Enter 0 (zero) if the answer is nil.

```
┌─────────────────────────┐
│                         │
└─────────────────────────┘
```

Calculate the allowable losses carried forward to the tax year 2022/23. Enter zero (0) if the answer is nil.

```
┌─────────────────────────┐
│                         │
└─────────────────────────┘
```

(c) Angela bought a warehouse as an investment, in May 2015 for £150,000. She spent £29,700 on enhancing the property in April 2017 and sold it for £290,000 in March 2022.

Angela made no other capital disposals in 2021/22.

She has taxable income of £26,145 in 2021/22.

Calculate Angela's capital gains tax liability for the tax year 2021/22 to the nearest pound.

```
┌─────────────────────────┐
│                         │
└─────────────────────────┘
```

60   LYNNETTE

(a)   **Select whether each of the following statements is true or false.**

Tick the appropriate box for each statement.

	True	False
An additional rate taxpayer does not have an annual exempt amount.		
Brought forward capital losses are offset after the annual exempt amount.		
Allowable losses can be transferred to a spouse or civil partner.		
Capital gains tax is paid at 38.1% on share gains made by an additional rate taxpayer.		

(b)   Lynnette sold her private residence making a gain of £360,000.

She had owned the house for 20 years.

The first 8 years she lived in the house and then as her employer relocated his business, she went to work in Scotland. She lived in rented accommodation in Scotland and never returned to her own house.

Calculate the capital gain on the sale of Lynnette's private residence.

_____

(c)   Kenneth had taxable income, after personal allowance, of £24,500 for the tax year 2021/22.

Kenneth had net gains for the tax year 2021/22 of £17,900.

Calculate Kenneth's capital gains tax for the tax year 2021/22.

_____

(d)   Candice made the following gains and losses in recent years:

Year	2019/20	2020/21	2021/22
Annual exempt amount £	12,000	12,300	12,300
Gains £	4,500	17,400	12,900
Loss £	18,300	3,200	1,200

Calculate the amount chargeable to capital gains tax for the tax year 2021/22. Enter 0 (zero) if the answer is nil.

_____

Calculate Candice's allowable losses carried forward to the tax year 2022/23. Enter 0 (zero) if the answer is nil.

_____

61 ALYSHA

(a) **Select whether each of the following statements is true or false.**

Tick the appropriate box for each statement.

	True	False
Current year allowable losses are deducted from current year gains, before the annual exempt amount is deducted.		
The rate of capital gains tax depends on the level of taxable income.		
Married couples and civil partners have one annual exempt amount between them.		
Gains made on disposals to a connected person can only be reduced by losses made on disposals to the same connected person.		

(b) Tony made the following gains and losses in recent years:

Year	Gains £	Losses £	Annual exempt amount £
2019/20	53,900	24,400	12,000
2020/21	2,500	19,200	12,300
2021/22	33,000	2,400	12,300

Calculate the amount chargeable to capital gains tax for the tax year 2021/22. Enter 0 (zero) if the answer is nil.

Calculate the allowable losses carried forward to the tax year 2022/23. Enter 0 (zero) if the answer is nil.

(c) Alysha bought a painting in May 2012 for £35,300, selling it in December 2021 for £52,000.

She paid auctioneers commission of 2% when she sold the painting and legal fees of £250 when she bought it.

Alysha has made no other capital disposals in the tax year 2021/22 and is a higher rate taxpayer.

She paid her accountant £100 to calculate her capital gains tax liability on this disposal.

Calculate Alysha's capital gains tax liability for the tax year 2021/22 in whole pounds.

62   TINEKE

(a)   **Select whether each of the following statements is true or false.**

Tick the appropriate box for each statement.

	True	False
All taxable gains of a basic rate taxpayer are taxed at 10%.		
Current year allowable losses must be deducted from current year gains, before any excess losses are carried forward.		
Gains on disposals to connected persons are taxed at the same rates of capital gains tax as gains on disposals to unconnected persons.		
The annual exempt amount is deducted from the capital gains tax for the tax year.		

(b)   Lissa made the following gains and losses in recent years:

Year	2019/20	2020/21	2021/22
Annual exempt amount £	12,000	12,300	12,300
Gains £	11,400	33,000	24,000
Loss £	14,500	1,300	4,700

Calculate the amount chargeable to capital gains tax for the tax year 2021/22. Enter 0 (zero) if the answer is nil.

```
[                    ]
```

Calculate Lissa's allowable losses carried forward to the tax year 2022/23. Enter 0 (zero) if the answer is nil.

```
[                    ]
```

(c)   Tineke bought a flat on 1 January 2013 for £99,000.

She lived in the flat until 31 December 2013 when she moved abroad to work for two years.

She then moved back into the flat on 1 January 2016 but this was short-lived and she moved out again to live with her boyfriend on 1 January 2017.

She sold the flat on 31 December 2021 for £169,000.

Calculate the capital gain on the sale of Tineke's flat.

```
[                    ]
```

(d)   Guy had taxable income, after personal allowance, of £34,500 for the tax year 2021/22.

Guy had net gains for the tax year 2021/22 of £27,000.

Calculate Guy's capital gains tax for the tax year 2021/22.

```
[                    ]
```

63   KIESWETTER

(a)   **Select whether each of the following statements is true or false.**

Tick the appropriate box for each statement.

	True	False
Private residence relief reduces the amount of gain chargeable on disposal of a main residence.		
The available annual exempt amount is reduced if gains exceed £100,000.		
A taxpayer can decide whether to deduct brought forward allowable losses from a gain in a tax year or carry the losses further forward.		
Unused annual exempt amount is wasted and cannot be used in other tax years.		

(b)   Ade made the following gains and losses in recent years:

Year	Gains £	Losses £	Annual exempt amount £
2019/20	55,000	24,500	12,000
2020/21	3,500	9,600	12,300
2021/22	18,600	2,000	12,300

Calculate the amount chargeable to capital gains tax for the tax year 2021/22. Enter 0 (zero) if the answer is nil.

```

```

Calculate the allowable losses carried forward to the tax year 2022/23. Enter zero (0) if the answer is nil.

```

```

(c)   Kieswetter has chargeable gains for the tax year 2021/22 of £40,300 and capital losses of £4,500. He also has capital losses brought forward of £6,700.

Kieswetter had taxable income (after deduction of the personal allowance) of £42,000 in the tax year 2021/22.

Calculate Kieswetter's amount chargeable to capital gains tax for the tax year 2021/22.

```

```

Calculate Kieswetter's capital gains tax for the tax year 2021/22.

```

```

INHERITANCE TAX

64 JANETTE

(a) Select whether each of the following statements connected to inheritance tax is true or false.

Tick the appropriate box for each statement.

	True	False
The annual exemption can be carried forward for one year but cannot be used until the annual exemption for the current year has been used.		
An exempt transfer may give rise to an inheritance tax liability if the donor dies within seven years.		
Chargeable lifetime transfers may give rise to two separate liabilities to inheritance tax.		
Taper relief will reduce a transfer of value made more than three but less than seven years prior to the donor's death.		
Where the donor of a potentially exempt transfer dies within seven years of making the gift, any inheritance tax due is payable by the donee.		

(b) Complete the following statements, selecting your answer from the list of options below each statement.

(i) Janette has never been married. She has not owned a property. The maximum nil rate band available when calculating inheritance tax on her death is _____.

Options
£175,000
£325,000
£500,000
£650,000

(ii) The rate of lifetime inheritance tax charged on a chargeable lifetime transfer (CLT) where the donor pays the tax is _____.

Options
20%
25%
40%
45%

(c)   In the situations set out below it should be assumed that no annual exemptions are available to the donor.

Tick the appropriate column for each of the gifts to indicate whether the gift is a chargeable lifetime transfer (CLT), a potentially exempt transfer (PET) or exempt.

Lifetime gift	CLT	PET	Exempt
£310 from Sharon to her husband.			
A house worth £510,000 to a trust.			
£4,000 from Maysoun to her grandson on his wedding day.			

65   FLORENCE

(a)   **Select whether each of the following statements in connection with inheritance tax is true or false.**

Tick the appropriate box for each statement.

	True	False
The small gifts exemption is £250 per donor per tax year.		
No IHT liability can arise in respect of a gift made more than seven years prior to death.		
An individual who has always lived in America and is not domiciled in the UK may still be liable to pay inheritance tax in the UK.		
The inheritance tax due in respect of the residue of a death estate is paid by the residuary legatee.		
The annual exemption cannot be deducted from the death estate even if there have been no gifts in the year of death.		

(b)   **Complete the following statements, selecting your answer from the list of options below each statement.**

(i)   Florence died in 2019. She used her full nil rate band on her death but none of her residence nil rate band. Florence's husband Logan died in 2021. The maximum amount of nil rate band and residence nil rate band that may be available when calculating the inheritance tax on Logan's death is _____.

Options
£500,000
£650,000
£675,000
£825,000

(ii)   The rate of taper relief that applies to inheritance tax on a gift made in May 2018 if the donor dies in April 2021 is _____.

Options
0%
20%
40%
60%
80%
100%

(c)   In the situations set out below it should be assumed that no annual exemptions are available to the donor.

Tick the appropriate column for each of the gifts to indicate whether the gift is a potentially exempt transfer (PET), a chargeable lifetime gift (CLT) or exempt.

Gift	PET	CLT	Exempt
A statue worth £830,000 from Eric to a national museum.			
£10,000 from Janine to her son.			
Gift of cash of £500,000 to a trust.			

66   ROWENA

(a)   Select whether each of the following statements in connection with inheritance tax is true or false.

Tick the appropriate box for each statement.

	True	False
Lifetime inheritance tax is charged at 25% on a chargeable lifetime transfer where the donor is paying the tax.		
An individual who is domiciled outside the UK is liable to IHT in respect of their worldwide assets.		
The annual exemption can be carried forward for one year and must be used before the annual exemption for the current year.		
A gift to a political party is an exempt transfer.		
The residence nil rate band is available on a lifetime gift of a residence from mother to son.		

(b) **Complete the following sentences using the words on the right.**

Tick the appropriate column for each of the sentences.

	20%	25%

(i) Rowena makes a lifetime gift to a trust. The trust pays the inheritance tax on the gift at a rate of ....

	may	will not

(ii) Ori gave £30,000 to his niece on 1 July 2013. In September 2021 Ori died.

The gift of £30,000 .... be subject to inheritance tax on Ori's death.

	may	will not

(iii) Umar gave £2,600 to his brother on 1 July 2019. This was his only gift in 2019/20. Gary died on 1 December 2021.

The gift of £2,600 .... be subject to inheritance tax on Umar's death.

(c) **Tick the appropriate column for each of the gifts to indicate whether the gift is a potentially exempt transfer (PET), a chargeable lifetime gift (CLT) or exempt.**

Gift	PET	CLT	Exempt
A painting worth £11,500 from Gomez to his civil partner.			
A sculpture worth £20,000 from James to his sister.			

67 JOSHUA

(a) **Select whether each of the following statements in connection with inheritance tax is true or false.**

Tick the appropriate box for each statement.

	True	False
Taper relief reduces the inheritance tax on death on a gift made between three and seven years earlier.		
Unused annual exemption can be transferred between spouses.		
A gift of £400 to a grandchild is reduced to £150 by the small gifts exemption.		
The rate of 40% applies for inheritance tax on death, whatever the level of the taxpayer's income.		
The residence nil rate band is deducted from the inheritance tax charged on a residence left to a direct descendant on death.		

(b)   **Complete the following sentences using the words on the right.**

Tick the appropriate column for each of the sentences.

	may	will not

(i)   Florence gave a house worth £430,000 to her son on 1 October 2015. Florence died on 1 May 2021.

The house .... be subject to inheritance tax in the UK following the death of Florence.

	would	would not

(ii)   Jemima gave £370,000 to a trust on 1 September 2012. In June 2021 Jemima died.

Inheritance tax .... have been charged on the gift when it was made.

	will	will not

(iii) Joshua is domiciled in France. He owns a house situated in the UK worth £675,000.

This house .... be subject to inheritance tax in the UK when Joshua dies.

(c)   **Tick the appropriate column for each of the gifts to indicate whether the gift is a potentially exempt transfer (PET), a chargeable lifetime gift (CLT) or exempt.**

Gift	PET	CLT	Exempt
Cash of £10,000 given from father to daughter for her 21st birthday.			
A sculpture worth £100,000 to the British Museum for national purposes.			

68   GAVIN

(a)   **Select whether each of the following statements in connection with inheritance tax is true or false.**

Tick the appropriate box for each statement.

	True	False
A marriage exemption on a gift from a brother to his sister is £1,000.		
A gift between two friends is not chargeable during the donor's lifetime.		
Taper relief of 60% is available to reduce the lifetime tax on a chargeable lifetime transfer (CLT) made between five and six years before the donor's death.		
The annual exemption for a tax year is always wasted if there are no gifts made during that year.		
The residence nil rate band may be available if a death estate includes a residence which is left to a direct descendant.		

(b) **Complete the following statements, selecting your answer from the list of options below each statement.**

(i) Denise died in March 2022. She was a basic rate taxpayer for income tax purposes in the tax year 2021/22. Inheritance tax on her death estate is paid at a rate of _____.

Options
7.5%
20%
25%
40%

(ii) Frieda made a chargeable lifetime transfer on September 2015. The rate of taper relief available on this transfer on her death in February 2022 is _____.

Options
0%
20%
40%
60%
80%
100%

(iii) Jonathan made a gift of £4,000 to his son in January 2021 and a gift of £10,000 to his daughter in May 2021. These are Jonathan's only lifetime gifts. The amount of annual exemption set against the May 2021 gift is _____.

Options
£3,000
£4,000
£5,000
£6,000

(c) **Tick the appropriate column for each of the gifts to indicate whether the gift is a potentially exempt transfer (PET), a chargeable lifetime gift (CLT) or exempt.**

Gift	PET	CLT	Exempt
Cash of £15,000 to a registered charity.			
Cash of £10,000 from a mother to her 12 year old son.			

69   MAISIE

(a)   **Select whether each of the following statements in connection with inheritance tax is true or false.**

Tick the appropriate box for each statement.

	True	False
Taper relief applied to the inheritance tax due on a gift on death can lead to a repayment of tax.		
A gift to charity is exempt up to an amount of £3,000. The excess is chargeable.		
Unused nil rate band of a civil partner who has died can be transferred to the surviving partner for use on the death of the surviving partner.		
The amount of the marriage exemption depends on the relationship between donor and donee.		
A chargeable lifetime transfer made more than seven years before the donor's death is not chargeable to inheritance tax on death.		

(b)   **Complete the following statements, selecting your answer from the list of options below each statement.**

(i)   Petra died on 31 December 2021. She had made no lifetime gifts during the tax year 2020/21 or the tax year 2021/22. The amount of annual exemption that can reduce Petra's chargeable death estate is _____.

Options
£0
£2,250
£3,000
£6,000

(ii)   Rob died in May 2021. His death estate included his home valued at £450,000. Rob had never married and left his estate to his brother on his death. The maximum amount of nil rate band and residence nil rate band that may be available on Rob's death is _____.

Options
£175,000
£325,000
£450,000
£500,000

(iii)   Inheritance tax paid on a particular chargeable lifetime transfer was charged at a rate of 20%. The tax was suffered by the _____(select from list 1) on the occasion of the _____ (select from list 2).

Options List 1	Options List 2
donor	gift
donee	donor's death

(c) **Tick the appropriate column for each of the gifts to indicate whether the gift is a potentially exempt transfer (PET), a chargeable lifetime gift (CLT) or exempt.**

Gift	PET	CLT	Exempt
Gift of £50,000 between civil partners			
Gift of £80,000 to a trust from an individual			

70 FRANCIS

(a) **Select whether each of the following statements in connection with inheritance tax is true or false.**

Tick the appropriate box for each statement.

	True	False
Gifts of cash of up to £250 between individuals are always exempt.		
A gift by any individual of £1,000 to someone getting married is exempt.		
The annual exemption reduces the tax due on a chargeable lifetime transfer by £3,000.		
The residence nil rate band may be available if a grandmother leaves a residence to her grandson on death.		
The annual exemption is applied to the first gift made in a tax year, even if this is a potentially exempt transfer.		

(b) **Complete the following statements, selecting your answer from the list of options below each statement.**

(i) Priti gave £7,000 to her daughter Siri on the occasion of Siri's marriage in January 2022. Priti has not made any other lifetime gifts. The amount of annual exemption that reduces the value of this gift is _____.

Options
£2,000
£3,000
£6,000
£7,000

(ii) Garth died in November 2021. His wife had died in 2018 and had left her entire estate to Garth. Neither Garth nor his wife made any lifetime transfers. The maximum amount of nil rate band and residence nil rate band that may be available on Garth's death is _____.

Options
£325,000
£500,000
£825,000
£1,000,000

(c)   **Tick the appropriate column for each of the gifts to indicate whether the gift is a potentially exempt transfer (PET), a chargeable lifetime gift (CLT) or exempt.**

Gift	PET	CLT	Exempt
Gift of £50,000 to a political party			
Gift of a car worth £12,000 to a friend			
Gift of assets worth £60,000 to a trust			

Section 2

ANSWERS TO PRACTICE QUESTIONS

PRINCIPLES AND RULES UNDERPINNING TAX

1   MICROMATTERS LTD

(a)   In order to comply with the fundamental principles set out in 'Professional conduct in relation to taxation' a tax adviser must:

–   be straightforward and honest in our professional and business relationships;

–   respect the confidentiality of information acquired as a result of professional and business relationships and, therefore, not disclose any such information to third parties without proper and specific authority, unless there is a legal or professional right or duty to disclose; and

–   comply with relevant laws and regulations and avoid any action that discredits the profession.

It is necessary to consider whether or not the request is valid. It should be borne in mind that the rules relating to HM Revenue and Customs' powers to obtain information are complex, such that it may be necessary to take specialist advice before responding.

Complying with a formal request and resolving the matter in a prompt manner should help to reduce the costs incurred.

A valid formal request for information overrides the duty of confidentiality and the firm must comply. The firm could be liable for civil or criminal penalties for non-compliance. However, a member must ensure that the confidentiality of information outside the scope of the request is maintained.

As long as we are not precluded from communicating with the client under the terms of the notice, the client should be advised of the notice and kept informed of progress and developments.

(b)   The principle of confidentiality remains. As the request is informal, the firm should direct the request either to the former client or to their agent, if the client gives permission.

Key answer tips

It is unlikely to be necessary to provide this level of detail in order to obtain the maximum marks in the assessment, however the examiner's feedback does often state that students do not commonly write enough on this task.

Most of this information can be found in the reference material so review this now to see where you can find the relevant material.

Taking a few minutes to brainstorm the areas to cover in your answer using your reference material can help you expand your answer in the exam and maximise your marks.

2   CORA

(a)   It is first necessary to establish the facts. We need to know if Cora sold a painting and, if so, the financial details of the sale.

If there is an undeclared chargeable gain, this is an error, which is unlikely to be trivial. It may be that our engagement letter allows us to disclose this to HMRC without specific authorisation from Cora. If it does we should do so.

If not, we must advise Cora to disclose the sale of the painting herself to HM Revenue and Customs immediately. We should advise her of any interest or penalties which may be imposed and the implications for her of not disclosing this information. We would originally do this orally then confirm this in writing.

If Cora refuses to disclose this information, we must cease to act for her. We should inform HM Revenue and Customs that we no longer act for her but we should not provide them with any reasons for our actions.

Key answer tips

Non-disclosure of a gain is an error. The Helpsheet on Dealing with Errors will help you to answer this question but it is important to apply the information to the scenario in the question.

(b)   Nisha has committed tax evasion as she has knowingly failed to provide information to HMRC to reduce her tax liability.

The guidelines advise that, while the firm cannot be involved in tax evasion itself, it can act for a client who is correcting their affairs as Nisha is doing here.

Key answer tips

The PCRT Helpsheet on Tax advice will help you to answer this question.

3   TOM

Key answer tips

Even a written question in your exam may have more than one part to it. You must scroll down and ensure you have answered the full question.

By using the reference material properly you should have easily been able to locate the information to answer part **(a)**.

It is important that you can distinguish between three terms in your exam:

1   Tax evasion – the use of illegal methods to reduce a tax liability

2   Tax avoidance – Methods of reducing tax which are legal but not following the intention of legislation

3   Tax planning – tax minimisation methods that are within the letter and the intention of tax legislation.

Part **(b)** of this question deals with these.

(a)   The primary responsibility for information in the returns falls to Tom as the taxpayer. He is responsible for ensuring that the returns filed contain complete and correct information to the best of his knowledge and belief.

The firm's responsibility is to ensure that the return is correct on the basis of the information provided by Tom. We should act in good faith in our dealings with HMRC, and in accordance with the principle of integrity, which requires us to be straightforward and honest in our business dealings.

If we act as a tax agent for Tom, the firm is not required to audit the figures in the books and records provided or verify information provided by either Tom or by a third party. However, we should take care not to be associated with the presentation of facts we know or believe to be incorrect or misleading and not to assert tax positions in a tax filing, which they consider to have no sustainable basis.

(b)   Tax evasion is the use of illegal methods to reduce a tax liability, for example the deliberate omission of income from the return. The firm should never be knowingly involved in tax evasion, although, of course, it is appropriate to act for a client who is rectifying their affairs.

Tax planning is using the tax legislation legally and as it was intended to minimise the tax liability whilst still paying the correct amount of tax. Tax avoidance is using methods of reducing tax which are legal but which do not use the law as it was intended. Under the Standards for tax planning members 'must not create, encourage or promote tax planning arrangements that (i) set out to achieve results that are contrary to the clear intention of Parliament in enacting relevant legislation and/or (ii) are highly artificial or highly contrived and seek to exploit shortcomings within the relevant legislation'. Such arrangements would be considered tax avoidance.

4   SOFIA

Key answer tips

The five key standards of tax planning are included in the reference material. These are very relevant for the PNTA syllabus so you must ensure you are happy with where to find them, and how to apply them to a question.

These are the main standards relevant for this scenario but you may pick up marks for discussing some of the others.

(a)   The Standards for tax planning should be considered in relation to any tax planning work carried out by the firm. The key standards to consider here appear to be:

- **Client Specific**

    Sofia has stated that this scheme can be used unaltered by many clients. The standards state that tax planning must be specific to the particular client's facts and circumstances. Clients must be alerted to the wider risks and implications of any courses of action.

- **Lawful**

    The interpretation of the law relied on here has not yet been proved in courts. Tax planning should be based on a realistic assessment of the facts and on a credible view of the law.

The firm should draw any client's attention to where the law is materially uncertain, as is the case here as HMRC is known to take a different view of the law. Members should consider taking further advice appropriate to the risks and circumstances of the particular case, for example, where litigation is likely.

(b)   The firm files as an agent and does not use the client's personal HMRC login details.

Agent passwords must be kept safe from unauthorised use and changed regularly.

Phishing emails should be forwarded to HMRC's phishing team without opening attachments or clicking on links.

The firm should have its own data protection and IT security policies.

5   TAX PRINCIPLES

(a)   Credit given for any TWO of the principles explained below.

The principle of neutrality does not apply here as the relief would not be equitable between different forms of businesses. By its nature, the proposal is designed to favour businesses with many employees who walk long distances as part of their jobs.

The principle of efficiency may not apply as the company would incur costs of the devices and also costs for time-consuming data collection and input.

The principle of certainty and simplicity does not seem to apply given the number of targets to be met, and a credit which is also dependent on profit rather than a set amount.

The principle of effectiveness and fairness may not apply, given the specific businesses the proposal benefits and if the targets are set too high to be reasonably met.

(b) Progressive taxes take an increasing proportion of income as income rises.

Regressive taxes take a decreasing proportion of income as income rises.

Proportional taxes take the same proportion of income as income rises.

Tutorial note

Income tax charged in the UK is progressive as the rate increase as income reaches certain bands.

---

6 CLARISSA

(a) To use the ties test, we need to know whether Clarissa was UK resident for one or more of the previous three tax years.

We also need to know how many days she spent in the UK in 2021/22.

If she was UK resident for one or more of the previous three tax years, then if she spent at least 46 days in the UK in 2021/22, she is UK resident.

If she was not UK resident in any of the previous three tax years, she is UK resident only if she spent at least 91 days in the UK.

Tutorial note

If someone is not automatically non-UK resident or UK resident, then look at whether they have sufficient ties to be UK resident. The number of ties and the number of days spent in the UK determine whether the individual is UK resident. It also depends on whether they were previously UK resident.

(b) Lewis would have UK deemed domicile in either of the following cases;

He was born in the UK with a UK domicile of origin and is UK resident.

He has been UK resident for at least 15 of the previous 20 years.

Tutorial note

Do not confuse residence and domicile.

The reference material gives much information useful to answering this task.

---

7   JOSEPH

(a)   As Joseph is UK resident, he will be charged income tax on his UK and his overseas income.

As Joseph is not UK domiciled or deemed domiciled, he can claim to use the remittance basis for his overseas income. This means he would only be charged income tax on his overseas income if it is brought into the UK.

Tutorial note

Whether someone is UK resident determines whether overseas income is charged to income tax. Whether someone is UK domicile determines the basis of this charge i.e. whether the arising basis or remittance basis applies.

(b)   Tax planning is using the tax legislation legally and as it was intended to minimise the tax liability whilst still paying the correct amount of tax. Tax avoidance is using methods of reducing tax which are legal but which do not use the law as it was intended. They might involve highly artificial or contrived steps to exploit loopholes in the law.

The use of charitable donations to reduce tax liabilities, including increasing the available personal allowance, is as intended by the law. Colette would be taking part in tax planning and not tax avoidance.

INCOME FROM EMPLOYMENT

8   SNAPE

(a)

	Snape	Sam
Percentage (%)	33	34
Car benefit £	7,258	9,180
Fuel benefit £	8,118	8,364

Workings

Snape's car

1   The CO_2 emissions are rounded down to 125g/km.

Appropriate percentage = 15% + 4% diesel + (125 − 55) × 1/5 = 33%

2   The benefit is based on the original list price of £21,995 and not the cost to the employer. The car benefit is £21,995 × 33% = £7,258

3   The fuel benefit is £24,600 × 33% = £8,118. The contributions to private fuel by Snape do not cover the cost of the private fuel and so the fuel benefit arises in full.

Sam's car

1   Appropriate percentage = 15% + 4% diesel + 1% + (125 − 55) × 1/5 = 34%

A further 1% applies as the car was registered before 6 April 2020

2   The car benefit is £27,000 × 34% = £9,180

3   The fuel benefit is £24,600 × 34% = £8,364

Key answer tips

Note that a mark would be given for the benefits based on the correct list prices if you calculated the benefit based on your answers to the percentages.

Tutorial note

Car benefits are calculated as:

Appropriate percentage × List price × n/12

Where n = number of months the car is available in the tax year.

The scale percentage is found from the following calculation:

15% + (CO₂ emissions − 55) × 1/5

- *CO₂ emissions are rounded down to the next number ending in 0 or 5.*

- *Diesel cars attract an extra 4% unless the car is RDE2 compliant.*

- *An addition 1% applies for cars registered before 6 April 2020.*

- *Maximum scale percentage is 37%.*

The car benefit covers all the running costs of the car except for the provision of private fuel and the services of a chauffeur. Costs such as repairs, insurance, servicing and road tax are not separately assessed on the employee. However, if an employee paid some of these expenses privately they could deduct the amount spent from their taxable car benefit.

Fuel benefit is calculated as follows:

- *Appropriate percentage × £24,600 × n/12*

- *Where n = number of months the benefit is available in the tax year.*

If an employee contributes towards the running costs of the car this is an allowable deduction, but partial contributions towards the cost of private fuel are NOT an allowable deduction.

(b)

Scenarios	£
On 6 December 2021, Loach was provided with a company loan for £7,000 on which he pays interest at 1.4% per annum.	0
Swift plc purchased a property for £100,000 in December 2015. In May 2016 the company spent £30,000 on an extension to the property. On 1 November 2020 an employee, Margarita, occupied the property. The market value of the property on 1 November 2020 was £220,000. The annual value of the property was £1,000.	2,100
Eve was provided with a flat (which was not job related) by her employer. The flat has an annual value of £6,000 and Eve's employer pays rent of £450 per month. Eve pays £100 per month towards the private use of the flat.	4,800

Working for Margarita

Expensive accommodation benefit

= ((£100,000 + £30,000) – £75,000) × 2% = £1,100

Total accommodation benefit including annual value

= £1,100 + £1,000 = £2,100

Tutorial note

Interest free and low interest loans which do not exceed £10,000 at any time in the tax year are an exempt benefit.

The house was purchased by Margarita's employers in December 2015 and Margarita moved in on 1 November 2020.

The house had therefore been owned by the employer for less than six years when Margarita first moved in.

Accordingly, the expensive accommodation benefit must be calculated using the original cost of the house plus improvements up to the start of the tax year, and not the market value when Margarita first moved in.

The house has been available for the whole of the tax year 2021/22, therefore there is no need to time apportion the benefit.

Working for Eve

		£
Higher of:	Annual value = £6,000, or	6,000
	Rent paid by employer = (£450 × 12) = £5,400	
Less: Rent paid by Eve (£100 × 12)		(1,200)
		———
Taxable benefit – 2021/22		4,800
		———

(c) True or false

	True	False
Dan is provided with furniture by his employer. Dan is taxed on 25% of the market value per annum		✓
Evan is provided with workplace childcare for his son. This is an exempt benefit	✓	
A loan of £12,000 provided to Frances in order that she can buy items wholly, exclusively and necessarily for her employment is exempt from income tax	✓	
Gerri will not be taxed on the reimbursement of expenses for home to work travel.		✓
Harry is provided with an eye test and spectacles for VDU use which are exempt benefits.	✓	

Tutorial note

Furniture provided by an employer is taxed on the employee at 20% per annum of the market value when first made available to the employee.

*Loans which do not exceed £10,000 at any time in the tax year **or** which are made to allow employees to purchase items wholly exclusively and necessarily for employment are an exempt benefit.*

The expense relating to travel from home to work represents ordinary commuting and is not tax allowable.

---

9 FRODO

(a)

	Frodo
Percentage (%)	26
Car benefit £	3,947
Fuel benefit £	4,264

Workings

1   The answer is 26%.

CO$_2$ emissions are rounded down to 110g/km.

Appropriate percentage = (15% petrol + (110 − 55) × 1/5) = 26%

Tutorial note

The car has CO$_2$ emissions in excess of 55g/km.

The appropriate percentage is therefore calculated in the normal way (i.e. a scale percentage of 15% for petrol cars and 19% for diesel cars, plus 1% for each 5 complete emissions above 55g/km up to a maximum percentage of 37%).

2   The answer is £3,947.

Car benefit = £26,000 × 26% × 8/12 (available from 5 August)

less £560 (contribution for private use)

3   The answer is £4,264.

Fuel benefit = (£24,600 × 26% × 8/12)

Tutorial note

Car benefits are calculated based on list price.

The £70 per month paid in respect of the private use of the car can be deducted from Frodo's car benefit. The total amount deductible is £70 per month for eight months.

The £30 per month partial contribution towards private fuel cannot be deducted from the fuel benefit.

(b)

Scenarios	£
On 2 June 2021 Yousef was provided by his employer with a laptop computer costing £750 for private use.	125
On 4 August 2021 Ian was provided by his employer with a van with a list price of £12,000 for private use. The van has zero CO_2 emissions. Ian is not provided with any private fuel.	0
On 6 April 2021 Siti left her employment. She took up the offer of purchasing a camera for £200 which she had been lent by her employer several years previously. This camera cost the company £500 and up to the end of the tax year 2020/21 Siti had been taxed on taxable benefits totalling £350. The camera was worth £250 at 6 April 2021.	50
Angel was provided with job related accommodation throughout the tax year 2021/22. This house cost her employers £125,000 in June 2019. The house has an annual value of £2,250. Angel's employer provided her with furniture at a cost of £10,000 and paid for the electricity bill which cost £1,200. Angel earns a salary of £22,000 for the tax year 2021/22.	2,200
Since 1 August 2021, Esme has lived in a house provided by her employer. This house cost her employers £175,000 in June 2014. The house has an annual value of £3,250 and Esme contributes £100 per month towards the cost of the benefit. The property had a market value of £228,000 when Esme moved in.	3,407

1 **Working for Yousef**

Use of asset benefit = (£750 × 20% × 10/12) = £125

Tutorial note

The benefit for use of a company asset such as a computer is 20% of the market value of the asset when first made available to the employee.

Yosef has only had use of the laptop for 10 months in the tax year 2021/22, therefore the benefit must be time apportioned.

2 **Benefit for Ian**

The answer is nil

Tutorial note

The benefit for use of a zero emission van is nil in the tax year 2021/22.

3 **Working for Siti**

Gift of asset after previous use of asset benefit = Higher of

(i)   (£250 – £200) = £50, or

(ii)   (£500 – £350 – £200) = £0

Tutorial note

When an asset previously used by an employee is sold or given to them the taxable benefit is calculated as follows.

Higher of:

(i)   Market value of asset at date of transfer to employee less price paid by employee

(ii)   Original market value when first supplied as a benefit less amounts taxed as a benefit to date less price paid by employee.

4 **Working for Angel**

	£
Ancillary benefits:	
Use of furniture (£10,000 × 20%)	2,000
Electricity bill	1,200
	–––––
	3,200
	–––––
Restricted to 10% of net earnings as job related	
(£22,000 × 10%)	2,200

Tutorial note

There is no basic charge or expensive accommodation benefit if the accommodation is job related.

5 Working for Esme

	£
Annual value	3,250
Additional charge for 'expensive' accommodation:	
(£228,000 − £75,000) × 2% (Note)	3,060
	6,310
Time apportion – from 1 August 2021 to 5 April 2022 (£6,310 × 8/12)	4,207
Less: Rent paid by Esme (£100 × 8 months)	(800)
Taxable benefit – 2021/22	3,407

Tutorial note

The house was purchased by Esme's employers in June 2014 and Esme moved in on 1 August 2021.

The house had therefore been owned by the employer for more than six years when Esme first moved in.

Accordingly, the expensive accommodation benefit must be calculated using the market value of the house when Esme first moved in rather than the original cost.

(c)

	True	False
The provision of a car parking space in a multi-storey car park near the place of work is an exempt benefit.	✓	
Free daily lunches provided to staff who have worked for the company for at least seven years are exempt benefits.		✓
The provision of a workplace nursery at the workplace is an exempt benefit.	✓	
An interest free loan of £9,000 is made on 6 April 2021 and written off on 5 April 2022. The write off of loan is an exempt benefit.		✓

Tutorial note

Subsidised meals are exempt benefits, but only provided they are available to staff generally. Therefore, only being available to staff who have worked for the company for at least seven years would make the benefit taxable, not exempt.

The provision of loans which total no more than £10,000 at any time in the tax year is exempt. However, loans of any amount which are written off are a taxable benefit.

10 BARRY

(a)

	Barry	Crouch
Percentage (%)	34	24
Car benefit £	6,880	2,800
Fuel benefit £	0	3,444

Workings for Barry

1. CO_2 emissions are rounded down to 125g/km.

   Appropriate percentage = (15% + 4% diesel + 1% + (125 − 55) × 1/5 = 34%

2. Cost of car

   = (Manufacturer's list price less capital contribution made by employee)

   but note that the maximum capital contribution deduction is £5,000.

   = (£27,000 − £5,000 max) = £22,000

3. Car benefit – car available throughout the whole of the tax year 2021/22

   = (£22,000 × 34%) less (£50 × 12) employee contribution

Tutorial note

For a car first provided before 6 April 2020 an additional 1% is added to the calculation of the appropriate percentage.

The car benefit covers all the running costs of the car except for the provision of private fuel and the services of a chauffeur.

Costs such as repairs, insurance, servicing and road tax are not assessed on the employee.

However, if an employee paid some of these expenses privately they could deduct the amount spent from their taxable car benefit.

Workings for Crouch

1. CO_2 emissions are rounded down to 100g/km.

   Appropriate percentage = (15% + (100 − 55) × 1/5 = 24%

2. Car benefit

   = £20,000 × 24% × 7/12 = £2,800

3. Fuel benefit = (£24,600 × 24% × 7/12) = £3,444

Tutorial note

The fuel benefit applies because Crouch receives private fuel (costing the employer £5,000 × 80% = £4,000) and does not reimburse his employer the whole cost (reimburses £1,000). Partial contributions towards private fuel are ignored.

The fuel benefit is based on a fixed figure of £24,600 in the tax year 2021/22.

The benefits are time apportioned because Crouch only has the car and fuel for 7 months during the tax year from 1 September 2021.

(b)

Scenarios	£
On 6 October 2021 Nikita was provided with a company loan of £28,000 on which she pays interest at 0.75% per annum.	175
Percy's employer provides him with a van for private use. The van has a market value of £20,000 and CO$_2$ emissions of 130g/km. Percy is not provided with any fuel for private use. Percy has the use of the van throughout the tax year 2021/22.	3,500
Molly was provided with a house (which is not job related) by her employer for the whole of the tax year 2021/22. The house has an annual value of £5,000 and cost Molly's employer £150,000 in September 2020. The house contains furniture costing £40,000. Heating bills of £750 per year are paid by her employer. Molly pays £200 per month towards the private use of the house.	12,850

1   **Working for Nikita**

Beneficial loan benefit = £28,000 × (2% – 0.75%) × 6/12 = £175

Tutorial note

Beneficial loan interest benefit is calculated as follows:

= Outstanding loan × the difference between the official rate of interest (2% in the tax year 2021/22) and the actual interest rate paid by the employee.

However, as the loan was provided for only six months of the tax year 2021/22, the benefit must be time apportioned as the rates of interest quoted are annual rates.

2   **Working for Percy**

A standard figure of £3,500 applies for the van benefit in the tax year 2021/22.

3   **Working for Molly**

	£
Annual value	5,000
Additional charge for 'expensive' accommodation:	
(£150,000 – £75,000) × 2%	1,500
Furniture (20% × £40,000)	8,000
Heating bills	750
	15,250
Less: Rent paid by Molly (£200 × 12)	(2,400)
Taxable benefit – 2021/22	12,850

(c)

	True	False
The payment of £800 fees for office employees attending computer skills courses is an exempt benefit.	✓	
An employer pays £500 for a smart phone for an employee. The employee will be taxed on this amount.		✓
Long service awards of £500 cash are given to employees completing 20 years' service. The employees will not be taxed on these awards.		✓ (Note i)
Health screenings for employees every six months. All health screenings are exempt benefits.		✓ (Note ii)

Tutorial note

(i)   *In order to be exempt, long service awards must be no more than £50 for each year of service provided service is at least 20 years. The award must not be in cash and the recipient must not have had an award within the previous 10 years. A cash award would be taxable.*

(ii)   *Only one health screening per year is exempt.*

11   JACKIE

(a)

	Jackie
Percentage (%)	28
Car benefit £	3,568
Fuel benefit £	0

Workings

1   CO_2 emissions are rounded down to 100g/km.

Appropriate percentage = (15% + 4% diesel + (100 – 55) × 1/5) = 28%

2   Cost of car = (£12,400 + £1,500 accessories) = £13,900. Car benefit = (£13,900 × 28% × 11/12)

3   Jackie reimburses the full cost of the private fuel so there is no fuel benefit.

Tutorial note

The cost of the car to use in the taxable benefit calculation is the manufacturer's list price plus the cost of accessories purchased with the car, and those added at a later date (unless the accessory cost less than £100).

For the car benefit to be reduced, it must be unavailable for at least 30 consecutive days. Temporary non-availability of less than 30 days is ignored.

Since the car was first provided on 1 May 2021, the benefit only applies for 11 months.

(b)

Scenarios	£
Gibbs is provided with accommodation by his employer, Tallmark plc. The property cost Tallmark plc £250,000 in May 2018 and the company spent £45,000 on improvements in June 2021. The property has an annual value of £6,500 and Gibbs pays rent of £150 per month to Tallmark plc. The property had a market value of £265,000 when Gibbs moved in on 20 December 2018.	8,200
Diego is provided with a house by his employer. The accommodation benefit is £2,600 before taking account of the following expenditure. The property was furnished by his employer at a cost of £20,000. The employer also paid for regular gardening and cleaning at the property which cost a total of £2,100 for the tax year 2021/22. In addition the employer spent £5,600 during the tax year 2021/22 on extending the garage.	8,700

Scenarios	£
During the tax year 2021/22 Betsy receives a £100 payment under her employer's staff suggestion scheme in respect of a proposal she made that reduced the costs incurred by the business. Her employer also pays her home telephone bills of £400 even though Betsy has no business use of the telephone.	400
Bismah's employer moved to larger premises which have a staff canteen available to all staff. Bismah is entitled to subsidised meals in the canteen for which she paid £1 per day for 250 days. The meals cost her employer £480 to provide.	0
Althea's employer made an interest-free loan to her of £16,000 on 1 April 2021. On 30 June 2021 Althea repaid £4,000 of the loan. Althea uses the average method of assessment.	280

1   **Working for Gibbs**

	£
Annual value	6,500
Additional charge for 'expensive' accommodation:	
(£250,000 – £75,000) × 2%	3,500
	————
	10,000
Less: Rent paid by Gibbs (£150 × 12)	(1,800)
	————
Taxable benefit – 2021/22	8,200
	————

Tutorial note

The accommodation was purchased by Gibbs's employers in May 2018 and Gibbs moved in on 20 December 2018. The accommodation had therefore been owned by the employer for less than six years when Gibbs first moved in. Accordingly, the expensive accommodation benefit must be calculated using the original cost of the house plus improvements up to the start of the tax year, and not the market value when Gibbs first moved in.

The improvements in June 2021 are not included in the calculations for the benefit for the tax year 2021/22 as they were incurred during the tax year, rather than before the start of the tax year. The cost of the improvements will however be included in next year's benefit calculation.

2   Working for Diego

	£
Accommodation benefit	2,600
Furniture benefit (£20,000 × 20%)	4,000
Household expenses (Note)	2,100
	─────
Taxable benefit – 2021/22	8,700
	─────

Tutorial note

The cost of extending the garage is not a taxable benefit as it is capital expenditure (i.e. an improvement to the property). It will be included in the cost of the property for the purpose of calculating any additional charge for expensive accommodation in the tax year 2022/23.

3   Working for Betsy

	£
Payment under staff suggestion scheme – exempt	—
Telephone expenses	400
	────
Taxable benefit – 2021/22	400
	────

Tutorial note

Payments made under a staff suggestion scheme of up to £5,000 are exempt benefits.

Telephone bills paid by the employer are taxable benefits valued at the cost to the employer.

4   Benefit for Bismah

The benefit for Bismah is £0.

Tutorial note

Provision of free or subsidised meals in a canteen is a tax free benefit provided there are canteen facilities for all staff.

5   Working for Althea

Benefit = ½ × (£16,000 + £12,000) × 2% = £280

Tutorial note

Under this method the benefit is calculated using the average loan balance. This is calculated as:

½ × (opening loan balance + closing loan balance)

The benefit is calculated as the average loan balance x official rate of interest (2% in the tax year 2021/22). Any interest paid by the employee would be deducted from the benefit.

(c)

	True	False
Arthur receives a mobile telephone for business and private use from his employer. Arthur is taxed on the private use portion of the costs.		✓
Brick Ltd provides a pool car at its factory for use by employees to travel around the site. This is an exempt benefit.	✓	
Colin is allowed use of a company van for a fortnight's camping holiday. There is no other private use. This is an exempt benefit.		✓

Tutorial note

The van benefit is taxable unless the private use by the employee is incidental. The use of the van for a fortnight would not be considered incidental private use.

12   SID

(a)

	Sid
Percentage (%)	32
Car benefit £	6,160
Fuel benefit £	5,248

Workings

1   CO_2 emissions are rounded down to 135g/km.

       Appropriate percentage = (15% + 0% diesel + 1% + (135 − 55) × 1/5) = 32%

2   Car benefit = (£30,000 × 32% × 8/12) − (£20 × 12) = £6,160

3   Fuel benefit = (24,600 × 32% × 8/12) = £5,248

Tutorial note

The car uses diesel but meets the RDE2 standard and so the additional 4% for diesel cars does not apply. The car was registered before 6 April 2020 and so an additional 1% does apply.

Since the car was only provided until 1 December 2021, the benefit only applies for 8 months.

(b)   **Calculate the taxable benefit provided to each employee in each scenario below for the tax year 2021/22. Round your benefit amounts to the nearest pound (£).**

Scenarios	£
On 6 October 2021, Bharat was provided with a loan of a home cinema system worth £3,600 by his employer. The cinema system is only used for private purposes.	360
Sybil was provided with a flat (which is not job related) by her employer. The flat has an annual value of £5,600 and Sybil's employer pays rent of £420 per month. Sybil pays £80 per month towards the private use of the flat.	4,640
Ben works for HF Ltd which provides its employees with fitness facilities on the company premises. The facilities are only open to employees. The annual running cost of the gym is £450 per employee. Ben uses the facilities once each week throughout the tax year 2021/22.	0
Bim's employer pays for his annual subscription at a health club near Bim's home. The subscription costs the employer £450 per annum.	450

1   **Working for Bharat**

       Use of asset benefit = (£3,600 × 20% × 6/12) = £360

Tutorial note

The benefit for the use of a company asset such as a home cinema system is 20% of the market value of the asset when first made available to the employee.

Bharat has only had use of the system for six months in the tax year 2021/22, therefore the benefit must be time apportioned.

2   Working for Sybil

		£
Higher of:	Annual value = £5,600, or	5,600
	Rent paid by employer = (£420 × 12) = £5,040	
Less: Rent paid by Sybil (£80 × 12)		(960)
Taxable benefit – 2021/22		4,640

3   Benefits for Ben and Bim

Ben has no taxable benefit. Bim has a benefit of £450.

Tutorial note

Provision of sport and recreational facilities open to staff but not the general public is an exempt benefit.

Payment of an employee's gym subscription of £450 would be taxed on the employee.

(c)

	True	False
A payment of £500 to an employee in accordance with the rules of the staff suggestion scheme is an exempt benefit.	✓	
Employees who work with computers can receive a free eye test organised by their employer, without being charged tax.	✓	
The funding of a Christmas party of £100 per employee in the tax year is a taxable benefit.		✓
A donation to a UK political party by an employee is an allowable expense reducing employment income.		✓

Tutorial note

The funding of a social event, such as a Christmas party, up to £150 per employee per tax year is an exempt benefit.

Political donations are not tax allowable.

13   JAYDEN

(a)

	Jayden
Percentage (%)	11
Car benefit £	3,520
Fuel benefit £	0

Workings

1   Appropriate percentage = 11%

2   Car benefit = (£37,000 – 5,000) × 11% = £3,520

Tutorial note

The car is a hybrid so the car benefit percentage depends on both the emissions and on the electric range.

(b)

Scenarios	£
Zamir is provided with a free annual health screening which costs the employer £350 per head.	0
Yasmin attended the annual staff party which cost £220 per head.	220
Graham received payments of £7 per night for 15 nights for personal expenses when staying away from home for work elsewhere in the UK.	105
Bailey had to relocate to a new town when he was promoted. His employer paid his removal expenses of £12,000.	4,000
When she was promoted to manager grade, Clare received a smart phone which cost her employer £380 per year.	0

Tutorial note

(i)   The cost of one annual health screening per year is an exempt benefit.

(ii)   Staff parties are only exempt if they cost no more than £150 per head.

(iii)   Personal expense payments up to £5 per night in the UK are exempt, but if the payments exceed this limit they are taxable.

(iv)   The first £8,000 of removal expenses is exempt.

(v)   One smart phones per employee is exempt.

(c)

	True	False
Sian was provided with accommodation by her employer three years after the property was purchased by the employer. The market value of the property is used to calculate the additional benefit.		✓
Jane received a non-cash long service award of £50 per year of her 25-year service. The award is tax free.	✓	
Ron uses his own car for business travelling. During the tax year 2021/22 he travelled 18,000 business miles for which he was paid 38p per mile by his employer. Ron can claim a tax allowable expense of £1,260.		✓

Working for Ron

	£
Received (18,000 × 38p)	6,840
Less: Allowable under HMRC rules:	
10,000 × 45p	(4,500)
8,000 × 25p	(2,000)
	———
Taxable employment income	340
	———

Tutorial note

The market value is used in the additional benefit calculation if the property is provided to the employee more than six years after the property was purchased. Otherwise the calculation uses the original cost, including additions prior to the start of the tax year.

Approved mileage allowance payments are 45p per mile for the first 10,000 business miles, and 25p for miles above this. This means Ron receives payments which exceed the approved allowance by £340.

14   MARIO

(a)

	Mario	Luke
Percentage (%)	37	4
Car benefit £	11,840	420
Fuel benefit £	9,102	0

Workings for Mario

1   CO_2 emissions are rounded down to 155g/km.

   Appropriate percentage = (15% + 4% diesel + 1% + (155 − 55) × 1/5 = 40%, but limited to 37%

2   Car benefit – car available throughout the whole year 2021/22

   = (£32,000 × 37%) = £11,840

3   Fuel benefit = (£24,600 × 37%) = £9,102

Tutorial note

For a car first provided before 6 April 2020 an additional 1% is added to the calculation of the appropriate percentage. For a diesel car which does not meet the RDE2 standard, a further 4% is added to the percentage. However, the maximum percentage is 37%.

Workings for Luke

1   CO_2 emissions are 1 − 50g/km. Electric range is 70 − 129 miles.

   Appropriate percentage = 4%

2   Cost of the car = list price less contribution up to £5,000

   = (£50,000 − £5,000) = £45,000

3   Car benefit – car available for three months

   = £45,000 × 4% × 3/12 − £30 = £420

Tutorial note

The car is a hybrid so the car benefit percentage depends on both the emissions and on the electric range.

The maximum capital contribution which can reduce the list price is £5,000.

The benefit is time apportioned because Luke only has the car for three months during the tax year from 5 January 2022.

The car benefit is reduced by Luke's contribution of £10 per month for three months.

(b)

Scenarios	£
During the tax year 2021/22 Tilly used her own car for her employment, driving 25,000 business miles. Her employer paid her 50 pence per mile for this.	4,250
Zoe's employer provided her with a van for private use, including private fuel. The van has a market value of £15,000 and CO$_2$ emissions of 140g/km. Zoe had the use of the van throughout the tax year 2021/22.	4,169
Lola had an interest-free loan from her employer of £18,000 outstanding on 6 April 2021. Lola paid back the full amount on 6 January 2022.	270
Jack was provided with a house (which is not job related) by his employer for the whole of the tax year 2021/22. The house has an annual value of £7,000 and cost Jack's employer £275,000 in February 2018 when it was first provided to Jack. An extension was built in January 2021 for £25,000. Jack pays £400 per month towards the private use of the house.	6,700

Working for Tilly

	£
Received (25,000 × 50p)	12,500
Less: Allowable under HMRC rules:	
10,000 × 45p	(4,500)
15,000 × 25p	(3,750)
	———
Taxable employment income	4,250
	———

Working for Zoe

The total van benefit is £4,169 (£3,500 + £669).

Working for Lola

Beneficial loan benefit = £18,000 × 2% × 9/12 = £270

Working for Jack

	£
Annual value	7,000
Additional charge for 'expensive' accommodation:	
(£275,000 + £25,000 − £75,000) × 2%	4,500
	———
	11,500
Less: Rent paid by Jack (£400 × 12)	(4,800)
	———
Taxable benefit – 2021/22	6,700
	———

Tutorial note

Approved mileage allowance payments are 45p per mile for the first 10,000 business miles, and 25p for miles above this.

The van benefit and fuel benefit are both set amounts which do not depend on emissions, except if the van were a zero-emission vehicle (then no benefit would arise).

The interest-free loan is outstanding for nine months and so the amount of the benefit is time apportioned.

The accommodation benefit includes the additional charge for 'expensive' accommodation. The cost used in this calculation includes the cost of the extension as this was incurred before the start of the tax year 2021/22.

(c)

	True	False
A car parking space provided at the company office for an employee is an exempt benefit.	✓	
An employer provides an employee with private use of a TV with market value £2,000. The benefit for the employee is £2,000.		✓
Sue's employer provides her with two mobile phones – one for her and one for her husband. Sue is not taxed on the provision of the phones.		✓
Anne attends one staff party in the tax year 2021/22. The party cost her employer £100 per employee. This is a taxable benefit.		✓

Tutorial note

The benefit on the provision of an asset for private use is 20% of the market value when provided.

Only one mobile phone is exempt. An employee is taxed on the provision of a second mobile phone.

A staff party costing up to £150 per year is exempt.

INCOME FROM INVESTMENT AND PROPERTY

15   SOPHIE

(a)   Sophie

	£
Taxable dividend income	4,700
£500 × 0% (dividend allowance in higher rate band)	0
£1,500 × 0% (dividend allowance in additional rate band)	0
£2,700 × 38.1%	1,029
Income tax liability	1,029

Serena

	£
Taxable savings income	4,300
£500 × 0% (savings allowance for a higher rate taxpayer)	0
£1,600 × 20% (remainder of basic rate band)	320
£2,200 × 40% (higher rate band)	880
Income tax liability	1,200

Tutorial note

Lottery winnings are exempt from tax.

(b)

Property	Letting and cost information	Taxable income £	Allowable expenses £
Flat	The furnished flat was let throughout the tax year 2021/22 with rent payable on the first of the month. The rent was £500 per month during 2021. On 1 January 2022 the rent was increased to £525 per month. Googoosh purchased a new corner sofa for the property for £1,800. A sofa similar to the old sofa would have cost £1,620. Googoosh was able to sell the old sofa for £130.	6,100	1,490
House	The unfurnished house was rented out for £480 per month, payable on the 10ᵗʰ of the month, but was empty until 1 November 2021 when a family moved in on a twelve month lease.	2,400	0

Workings

	Income £	Expenses £
Flat:		
(£500 × 8) + (£525 × 4)	6,100	
New sofa (Note) (£1,620 – £130)		1,490
House:		
(£480 × 5)	2,400	

Tutorial note

In the absence of any election and where gross rents are less than £150,000, property income will be assessed on the cash basis. Therefore the rent on the flat is assessed based on the amounts received during the tax year (£500 for May to December and £525 for January to April).

A deduction is available for the cost of replacing the sofa with a similar item. The allowable amount is reduced by any proceeds from the sale of the original sofa.

The property allowance is not relevant in this question as both the rent received and the expenses exceed £1,000.

(c)

	True	False
Giorgis has bought a house which he intends to let furnished. The initial cost of providing the furniture will be an allowable cost when calculating taxable property income.		✓
Income from property is always taxed on the cash basis unless the taxpayer elects to use the accruals basis.		✓

Tutorial note

The first statement is false because it is only the cost of replacing domestic items that is allowable and not the cost of the original items.

The second statement is false because the cash basis is only automatic for taxpayers with gross rents not exceeding £150,000 (though these taxpayers can elect to use accruals basis instead). For taxpayers with gross rents exceeding this figure the accruals basis applies.

16 CASTILAS

(a) Castilas

	£
Taxable dividend income £(18,000 – 12,570)	5,430
	——
£2,000 × 0% (dividend allowance)	0
£3,430 × 7.5%	257
	——
Income tax liability	257
	——

Hannah

	£
Taxable savings income	8,900
	——
£500 × 0% (savings allowance for a higher rate taxpayer)	0
£8,400 × 40% (higher rate)	3,360
	——
Income tax on savings income	3,360
	——

(b)

Property	Letting and cost information	Taxable income £	Allowable expenses £
House	The unfurnished house is rented out for £1,000 per month. The property was occupied until 1 September 2021 when the tenants suddenly moved out, owing the rent for August. Sunita knows she will not recover this rent. The property was let again from 1 December 2021. The rent is received on the first of each month. Sunita incurred 5% commission to the agent on rent received. This was deducted from each monthly rent payment.	8,000	400
Flat	The furnished flat is rented out for £600 per month. The property was occupied by Sunita during April 2021. She then started looking for a tenant, but the property was unoccupied until 1 July when a couple moved in on a twelve-month lease. The rent was received on the 8th of each month. In May 2021, Sunita purchased new lounge furniture for the property for £2,000 and dining furniture for £1,200. Lounge furniture similar to the old furniture could have been purchased for £1,100. Sunita sold the old lounge furniture for £180. The property did not have any dining furniture prior to the purchase in May.	5,400	920

Workings

	Income £	Expenses £
House:		
(£1,000 × 5) + (£1,000 × 4)	9,000	
Less: Irrecoverable debt relief	(1,000)	
	─────	
	8,000	
Commission (£8,000 × 5%)		400
Flat:		
(£600 × 9)	5,400	
New lounge furniture (£1,100 – £180)		920
New dining furniture		0
		─────
		920
		─────

Tutorial note

The question states that Sunita has elected to be taxed on the accruals basis therefore the actual dates of receipt and payment are not relevant.

All of the rent accrued should be brought into the computation, however, there is relief for the August rent which is irrecoverable.

Note that the entry for rental income is for the net rents actually received (i.e. £8,000 in this case) rather the figure for rents accrued (£9,000) and the £1,000 irrecoverable debt deduction has not been included as an expense.

A deduction is available for the cost of replacing the lounge furniture with a similar item. The allowable amount is reduced by any proceeds from the sale of the original furniture.

No deduction is available for the dining furniture as this is not a replacement item, but is the initial purchase of a capital item.

The property allowance is not relevant in this question as both the rent received and the expenses exceed £1,000.

(c)

	True	False
Property losses from furnished lettings can be deducted from profits on unfurnished lettings.	✓	
Dividends received from an ISA are always exempt from tax.	✓	

Tutorial note

The first statement is true because net rental income is found by netting off all the rental profits and losses of the year, irrespective of whether the properties are furnished or unfurnished.

Income received from an ISA is exempt.

17   RAMOS

(a)   Ramos

£2,000 is taxed at 0% (dividend allowance).

Basic rate band remaining = £37,700 – £26,300 – £2,000 = £9,400. This amount is taxed at 7.5%.

Tutorial note

The first £2,000 of taxable dividend income is always covered by the dividend allowance, but this amount still falls within the basic rate band. The remaining basic rate band gives the amount taxable at 7.5%

Pete

	£
Taxable savings income	1,400
£1,400 × 45% (additional rate)	630
Income tax on savings income	630

Tutorial note

As Pete's total taxable income exceeds £150,000 he is an additional rate taxpayer meaning he does not have a savings allowance.

(b)

Property	Letting and cost information	Taxable income £	Allowable expenses £
Cottage	The furnished cottage is rented out for £500 per month. All rent was received during the tax year. Will pays gardeners fees of £50 a month and cleaners bills of £70 a month. He also paid for repairs costing £400. All amounts were paid during the tax year, except for the last month's cleaner's fees.	6,000	1,770
Flat	The furnished flat is rented out for £3,600 per year. The property was unoccupied until 1 July 2021. Rent is paid monthly in arrears. Will paid water rates of £500 and insurance of £500 in respect of the flat for the tax year 2021/22 in May 2021.	2,700	1,000

Workings

	Income £	Expenses £
Cottage:		
(£500 × 12)	6,000	
Gardening (£50 × 12)		600
Cleaning (£70 × 11)		770
Repairs		400
		———
Allowable expenses		1,770
Flat:		
(£3,600 × 9/12)	2,700	
Expenses:		
Water rates		500
Insurance – flat		500
		———
Allowable expenses		1,000

Tutorial note

In the absence of any election and where gross rents are less than £150,000, property income will be assessed on the cash basis.

The cleaner has only been paid for 11 months work during the tax year.

The property allowance is not relevant in this question as both the rent received and the expenses exceed £1,000.

(c)

	True	False
When calculating an individual's property income any costs of improving the property are not allowable.	✓	
Property losses can be offset against an individual's total income in the tax year.		✓

Tutorial note

The first statement is true because improvements to the property are capital expenditure and are therefore not allowable.

The second statement is false because property losses can only be set against future property income, not the total income in the current tax year.

18   MARLON

(a)   Marlon

	£
Taxable dividend income (£3,300 – £1,500)	1,800
£1,800 × 0% (dividend allowance)	0
Income tax liability	0

Dean

	£
Taxable savings income	8,300
£500 × 0% (savings allowance for a higher rate taxpayer)	0
£7,800 × 40% (higher rate band)	3,120
Income tax liability	3,120

(b)

Property	Letting and cost information	Taxable income £	Allowable expenses £
House	The unfurnished house is rented out for £7,200 per annum, payable on the first of the month. The property was occupied until 28 February 2022 when the tenants suddenly moved out, without paying the rent for February. Edward moved in for the month of March before the property was let again from 1 April 2022 to another family. Edward paid £700 for council tax during the year.	6,000	642
Bungalow	The furnished bungalow is rented out for £550 per month, receivable on the 6th of the month. The property was unoccupied until 6 October 2021. Edward purchased a new sofa for the property for £2,100. A sofa similar to the old one would have cost £900. Edward sold the old sofa for £220.	3,300	680

Workings

	Income £	Expenses £
House:		
(£7,200 × 10/12)	6,000	
Council tax (£700 × 11/12)		642
Bungalow		
(£550 × 6)	3,300	
New sofa (£900 – £220)		680

Tutorial note

In the absence of any election and where gross rents are less than £150,000, property income will be assessed on the cash basis. Therefore the rent on the house is assessed based on the amounts received during the tax year (allowing relief for the unpaid rent for February and taxing the rent paid on 1 April 2022).

Only 11/12 of the council tax expense on the house is allowable as Edward was in the property for the month of March.

A deduction is available for the cost of replacing the sofa with a similar item. The allowable amount is reduced by any proceeds from the sale of the original sofa.

The property allowance is not relevant in this question as both the rent received and the expenses exceed £1,000.

(c)

	True	False
Property expenses incurred when the property is empty cannot be deducted from property income, even if the property is available to let.		✓
In 2021/22 the maximum amount that Taran (aged 42) can invest in an ISA is £1,000.		✓

Tutorial note

The first statement is false as property expenses can always be deducted from property income as long as the property is available to let and the expenses are incurred wholly and exclusively for the purposes of the property business.

The maximum that an individual aged 18 or over can invest in an ISA in 2021/22 is £20,000. This figure covers total investments in all ISA products for the year.

Note that those aged 16 and over can invest in a cash only ISA, however only those aged 18 or over can invest in a stocks and shares ISA.

---

19 HUANG

(a) Michelle

	£
Taxable dividend income	2,600
£2,000 × 0% (dividend allowance for a higher rate taxpayer)	0
£600 × 32.5%	195
Income tax liability	195

Huang

	£
Taxable savings income	5,700
£0 × 0% (no savings allowance for additional rate taxpayer)	0
£3,500 × 40% (£150,000 – £146,500)	1,400
£2,200 × 45% (additional rate band)	990
Income tax liability	2,390

(b) Rebecca's rental income under the accruals basis is £10,200.

Working

	15 Olden Way	**29 Harrow Crescent**	**Total**
	£	£	£
Income:			
(£600 × 12 months)	7,200		
(£500 × 6 months)		3,000	
Rental income			10,200

Rebecca's allowable expenses under the accruals basis are £1,783.

	15 Olden Way	**29 Harrow Crescent**	**Total**
	£	£	£
Expenses:			
Roof repair		1,500	
Insurance			
(£150 × 9/12 + £180 × 3/12)	158		
(£120 × 9/12 + £140 × 3/12)		125	
Expenses			1,783

Tutorial note

The question states that Rebecca has elected to be taxed on the accruals basis therefore the actual dates of receipt and payment are not relevant.

*Expenses are allowable on an accruals basis; therefore the insurance **accrued** in the tax year should be brought into the computation. It is therefore necessary to time apportion the expense.*

The property allowance is not relevant in this question as both the rent received and the expenses exceed £1,000.

(c)

	True	False
The property allowance is always automatically applied, although the taxpayer can elect not to claim it		✓
Ben, a landlord, delays paying a March repair bill until 15 April 2022. He can deduct this bill from his property income for the tax year 2021/22 whether he uses the accruals basis or the cash basis.		✓

Tutorial note

The property allowance is only automatically applied when gross rental income is £1,000 or less.

A bill incurred in March 2022 but paid in April 2022 can be deducted in the tax year 2021/22 if the accruals basis is used. Under the cash basis, expenses are only allowed when paid.

20   RAVI

(a)

	£
Taxable dividends	14,000
Tax payable on dividend income	900
Tax payable on savings income	290

Tutorial note

Ravi's trading profits are taxable as non-savings income. They use his personal allowance so the taxable amount of these is £9,430 (£22,000 – £12,570).

The dividends received from an ISA are exempt.

Ravi's total taxable income is £25,880 (£9,430 + £2,450 + £14,000), meaning he is a basic rate taxpayer.

When taxing his savings income he will get a savings allowance of £1,000. The tax is therefore £1,450 (£2,450 – £1,000) at 20%, giving £290.

When taxing his dividend the first £2,000 will be covered by the dividend allowance. The tax on the balance is calculated at 7.5%, giving £900 (£12,000 x 7.5%)

(b)   Wilma's rental income is £3,000 (£3,600 × 10/12).

Wilma's allowable expenses are £1,000.

Tutorial note

In the absence of any election and where gross rents are less than £150,000, property income will be assessed on the cash basis. Therefore, the rent on the flat is assessed based on the amounts received during the tax year, i.e. 10 months of rent.

The insurance costs paid during the year are allowable but as the property allowance exceeds this, the property allowance should be claimed instead.

Redi's rental income is £3,750 (£750 × 5 months).

Redi's allowable expenses are £1,092 (£900 + (£160 × 8/12) + £85)

Tutorial note

The question states that Redi has elected to be taxed on the accruals basis therefore the actual dates of receipt and payment are not relevant.

*Expenses are allowable on an accruals basis; therefore the insurance **accrued** in the tax year should be brought into the computation. It is therefore necessary to time apportion the expense.*

The property allowance is not relevant in this question as both the rent received and the expenses exceed £1,000.

(c)

	True	False
A taxpayer with gross rental income of more than £1,000 and expenses of less than £1,000 should always claim the property allowance	✓	
Interest from NS&I Savings Certificates is exempt.	✓	

Tutorial note

A taxpayer with property income over £1,000 has a choice of being assessed on:

1   *Gross rents less expenses; or*

2   *Gross rents less £1,000 (property allowance).*

In exam questions where gross rents exceed £1,000 you should deduct the property allowance instead of expenses if these are less than £1,000 (as this will give the lower amount of assessable income).

21   HOWARD

(a)   Wilf

	£
Taxable dividend income	5,000
£2,000 × 0% (dividend allowance for a higher rate taxpayer)	0
£3,000 × 7.5% (basic rate band)	225
Income tax liability	225

Wilf's basic rate band remaining = £37,700 – (£45,000 – £12,570) = £5,270, so the total dividend of £5,000 is within this.

Jamie

	£
Taxable savings income	3,950
£500 × 0% (savings allowance)	0
£3,450 × 40% (higher rate band)	1,380
Income tax liability	1,380

(b) Howard's deductible mileage expenses are £4,750.

Working

	£
10,000 miles at 45p per mile	4,500
1,000 miles at 25p per mile	250
	4,750

Tutorial note

Mileage allowances for residential landlords are calculated using the approved mileage allowance rates provided in the assessment. Note that these can be claimed for the purposes of managing the rental properties only.

Howard's rental income is £93,000

Working

	£
8,000 × 12	96,000
Less: Amounts not received during 2021/22	(3,000)
	93,000

Rosalie's allowable insurance expense is £2,070.

Working

Insurance expense = (£1,800 × 3/12) + (£2,160 × 9/12) = £2,070

Tutorial note

Rosalie is assessed on the accruals basis as her gross rents exceed £150,000.

(c) Tick one box on each line.

	True	False
Losses made on renting out a property can only be offset against property profits.	✓	
Any property losses which cannot be offset in the year they are incurred cannot be carried forward.		✓

Tutorial note

Losses made on renting out a property can only be offset against property profits. If a taxpayer has more than one rental property profits and losses on individual properties can be netted off. If the taxpayer makes an overall loss they show property income for the year of £Nil then carry forward this loss against future property income only.

Property losses which cannot be offset in the year they are incurred are carried forward against future property income profits. This treatment is automatic. Brought forward losses are offset against future property income profits as soon as possible.

INCOME TAX PAYABLE

22 FENFANG

Income tax computation – 2021/22

	Non-savings	Dividends	Total
	£	£	£
Employment income	70,000		70,000
Dividends		40,200	40,200
	———	———	———
Net income	70,000	40,200	110,200
Less: Adjusted PA (W1)	(8,820)		(8,820)
	———	———	———
Taxable income	61,180	40,200	101,380
	———	———	———

Income tax:

Non-savings – basic rate	40,400 × 20% (W2)	8,080
Non-savings – higher rate	20,780 × 40%	8,312
	61,180	
Dividends – dividend allowance	2,000 × 0%	0
Dividends – higher rate	38,200 × 32.5%	12,415
	101,380	

Income tax liability	28,807
Less: Tax credit	
PAYE	(15,500)
Income tax payable	13,307

Workings

(W1) Adjusted personal allowance

	£		£
Personal allowance			12,570
Net income	110,200		
Less: PPC (£2,000 × 100/80)	(2,500)		
Gift aid (£160 × 100/80)	(200)		
Adjusted net income	107,500		
Less: Limit	(100,000)		
Excess	7,500	× 50%	(3,750)
Adjusted PA			8,820

(W2) Extended basic and higher rate bands

	BR band £	HR band £
Basic rate/Higher rate bands	37,700	150,000
Plus: PPC (£2,000 × 100/80)	2,500	2,500
Gift aid (£160 × 100/80)	200	200
Extended bands	40,400	152,700

Tutorial note

As Fenfang's adjusted net income exceeds £100,000, her personal allowance must be reduced.

Adjusted net income = net income less gross gift aid donations and gross personal pension contributions.

As Fenfang has made both a personal pension payment and gift aid donation, her 'adjusted net income' needs to be calculated and compared to the £100,000 limit.

In addition, her basic rate and higher rate bands need to be extended by the gross personal pension contribution and gift aid donation to determine the appropriate rate of tax to apply.

As her income falls below the extended £152,700 additional rate threshold, her income in excess of £40,400 is taxed at 40% (non-savings income) and 32.5% (dividends).

All taxpayers are entitled to a dividend allowance of £2,000.

23   MARYAM

Income tax computation – 2021/22

		Total
		£
Property income	(£48,000 – £600)	47,400
Interest		250
ISA		0
Dividends		14,000
Net income		61,650
Less: PA		(12,570)
Taxable income		49,080

Income tax:		
Non-savings – basic rate	34,830 × 20%	6,966
Savings – savings allowance	250 × 0%	0
Dividends – dividend allowance	2,000 × 0%	0
Dividends – basic rate (W)	1,220 × 7.5%	92
Dividends – higher rate	10,780 × 32.5%	3,504
	49,080	
Income tax payable		10,562

Tutorial note

Maryam's property loss is automatically deducted from her property income. The net figure is assessable as non-savings income.

The personal allowance is deducted from non-savings income in priority to her savings and dividend income. The taxable non-savings income is £34,830 (£47,400 – £12,570).

Working: Extended basic rate band

	£
Basic rate band	37,700
Plus: Gift aid (£40 × 100/80 x 12)	600
Extended basic rate band	38,300

Tutorial note

Maryam's basic rate band can be extended by the gross amount of her gift aid donations.

Although her income falling within the savings and dividend allowances is taxable at 0%, this income uses up the basic rate band in priority to other dividend income.

The basic rate band remaining for the dividends is calculated as:

£38,300 – £34,830 – £250 – £2,000 = £1,220

Tommy

Income tax computation – 2021/22

		Total
		£
Employment income	(£80,000 – 5% × £80,000)	76,000
Interest		3,000
Dividends		1,000
Net income		80,000
Less: PA		(12,570)
Taxable income		67,430

Income tax:

Non-savings – basic rate	37,700 × 20%	7,540
Non-savings – higher rate	25,730 × 40%	10,292
Savings – savings allowance	500 × 0%	0
Savings – higher rate	2,500 × 40%	1,000
Dividends – dividend allowance	1,000 × 0%	0
	———	
	67,430	
	———	
Income tax liability		18,832
Less: PAYE		(17,000)
		———
Income tax payable		1,832
		———

Tutorial note

Tommy's contribution to his employer's occupational pension scheme is deducted from his salary to give employment income.

The personal allowance is deducted from non-savings income in priority to his savings and dividend income. The taxable non-savings income is £63,430 (£76,000 – £12,570) of which £25,730 (£63,430 – £37,700) is taxed at the higher rate.

Key answer tips

In the exam you could be provided with a grid consisting of either three or five columns so you must be prepared to deal with either situation.

If faced with three columns a useful approach is to write up the full five column approach on paper then type up the total column into the grid in your exam.

Remember you will not be able to include totals lines in your answer but do not worry about this, the marker will be able to follow when you are adding down as long as your answer is clearly labelled.

24   LUCIA

Income tax computation – 2021/22

	Non-savings	Savings	Dividends	Total
	£	£	£	£
Employment income	40,000			40,000
Lottery winnings	0			0
Savings income		800		800
Dividends			18,000	18,000
Net income	40,000	800	18,000	58,800
Less: PA	(12,570)			(12,570)
Taxable income	27,430	800	18,000	46,230

Income tax:

Non-savings – basic rate	27,430 × 20%	5,486
Savings – savings allowance	500 × 0%	0
Savings – basic rate	300 × 20%	60
Dividends – dividend allowance	2,000 × 0%	0
Dividends – basic rate	8,470 × 7.5%	635
Dividends – higher rate	7,530 × 32.5%	2,447
	46,230	
Income tax liability		8,628
Less: PAYE		(7,900)
Income tax payable		728

Tutorial note

Lucia is a higher rate taxpayer as her total taxable income exceeds £37,700. This means she is entitled to a savings allowance of £500.

Working: Extended basic rate band

	£
Basic rate band	37,700
Plus: Gift aid (2% × £40,000 × 100/80)	1,000
Extended basic rate band	38,700

Tutorial note

Lucia's basic rate band can be extended by the gross amount of her personal pension contributions.

Gareth

Income tax computation – 2021/22

	Non-savings	Savings	Dividends	Total
	£	£	£	£
Self-employment income	160,000			160,000
Savings income		580		580
Dividends (£30,000 – £17,000)			13,000	13,000
Net income	160,000	580	13,000	173,580
Less: PA	(0)			(0)
Taxable income	160,000	580	13,000	173,580

Income tax:			
Non-savings – basic rate	37,700 × 20%		7,540
Non-savings – higher rate	112,300 × 40%		44,920
Non-savings – additional rate	10,000 × 45%		4,500
Savings – additional rate	580 × 45%		261
Dividends – dividend allowance	2,000 × 0%		0
Dividends – additional rate	11,000 × 38.1%		4,191
	173,580		
Income tax payable			61,412

Tutorial note

Gareth is an additional rate taxpayer as his total taxable income exceeds £150,000. This means he is not entitled to a savings allowance.

Key answer tips

It is important when using this type of layout to analyse the taxable income into 'non-savings income', 'savings' and 'dividends' as different rates of tax apply to the different sources of income.

Note that:

- The above layout should be possible if the CBA gives at least four columns to complete the calculation.

- The total lines do not have to be inserted in the real CBA.

- You may find it useful to do the computation on paper first before inputting on screen.

- If the source of income is not specified in the CBA, always assume it is 'non-savings income'.

- It is acceptable to have the total column on the right rather than on the left if you prefer. However, we recommend that the analysis columns are in the fixed order: 'non-savings income', 'savings' and then 'dividends', as this is the order in which they must be taxed through the bands. Nil columns are not required.

25 ROMAN

Income tax computation – 2021/22

	Non-savings £	Savings £	Dividends £	Total £
Pension	23,696			23,696
Property income (£4,300 – £1,300)	3,000			3,000
Savings income		2,720		2,720
Dividends			6,144	6,144
Net income	26,696	2,720	6,144	35,560
Less: PA	(12,570)			(12,570)
Taxable income	14,126	2,720	6,144	22,990

Income tax:		
Non-savings – basic rate	14,126 × 20%	2,825
Savings – savings allowance	1,000 × 0%	0
Savings – basic rate	1,720 × 20%	344
Dividends – dividend allowance	2,000 × 0%	0
Dividends – basic rate	4,144 × 7.5%	311
	22,990	
Income tax liability		3,480

Tutorial note

Roman's pension income is taxable income and is treated as earned 'non-savings income'.

As Roman is a basic rate taxpayer he is entitled to a savings allowance of £1,000. All taxpayers are entitled to a dividend allowance of £2,000.

Alison

Income tax computation – 2021/22

		Total £
Self-employment income		113,000
Net income		113,000
Less: PA (W)		(12,570)
Taxable income		100,430
Income tax:		
Non-savings – basic rate	50,950 × 20%	10,190
Non-savings – higher rate	49,480 × 40%	19,792
	100,430	
Income tax liability		29,982

Workings

(W1) Adjusted personal allowance

	£	£
Personal allowance		12,570
Net income	113,000	
Less: PPC (£800 × 12 × 100/80)	(12,000)	
Gift aid (£1,000 × 100/80)	(1,250)	
Adjusted net income	99,750	
Full PA available as ANI < £100,000		12,570

(W2) Extended basic rate band

	BR band £
Basic rate	37,700
Plus: PPC (£800 × 12 × 100/80)	12,000
Gift aid (£1,000 × 100/80)	1,250
Extended band	50,950

Tutorial note

Alison's income exceeds £100,000, so her personal allowance may be reduced. However, it is Alison's adjusted net income that needs to be compared to the £100,000 limit.

Adjusted net income = net income less gross gift aid donations and gross personal pension contributions.

As Alison's adjusted net income is lower than £100,000, she receives the full personal allowance.

In addition, her basic rate band need to be extended by the gross personal pension contribution and gift aid donation to determine the appropriate rate of tax to apply.

26   RAY

Income tax computation – 2021/22

	Non-savings £	Savings £	Total £
Income (£120,870 – £10,000)	110,870		110,870
Savings income (£3,900 – £200)		3,700	3,700
Net income	110,870	3,700	114,570
Less: PA (W1)	(5,535)		(5,535)
Taxable income	105,335	3,700	109,035

Income tax:			
Non-savings – basic rate	38,200 (W2) × 20%		7,640
Non-savings – higher rate	67,135 × 40%		26,854
Savings – savings allowance	500 × 0%		0
Savings – higher rate	3,200 × 40%		1,280
	109,035		
Income tax liability			35,774
Less: PAYE			(34,000)
Income tax payable			1,774

Tutorial note

The pension contribution made by Ray's employer is not taxable. Ray's contribution to the occupational pension scheme is assumed to be made under net pay arrangements and reduces his employment income.

As Ray is a higher rate taxpayer he is entitled to a savings allowance of £500. The interest received from the ISA is exempt.

Workings

(W1) Adjusted personal allowance

	£		£
Personal allowance			12,570
Net income	114,570		
Less: Gift aid (£400 × 100/80)	(500)		
	———		
Adjusted net income	114,070		
Less: Limit	(100,000)		
	———		
Excess	14,070	× 50%	(7,035)
	———		———
Adjusted PA			5,535
			———

(W2) Extended basic rate band

	£
Basic rate band	37,700
Plus: Gift aid (£400 × 100/80)	500
	———
Extended basic rate band	38,200
	———

Tutorial note

As Ray's adjusted net income exceeds £100,000, his personal allowance must be reduced.

Adjusted net income = net income less gross gift aid donations and gross personal pension contributions.

As Ray has made a gift aid donation, his 'adjusted net income' needs to be calculated and compared to the £100,000 limit. His net income has already been reduced by the pension contribution to the occupational pension scheme under net pay arrangements, and so no further reduction is made for this.

In addition, Ray's basic rate band needs to be extended by the gross gift aid donation to determine the appropriate rate of tax to apply.

27   JJ

Income tax computation – 2021/22

	Non-savings £	Savings £	Dividends £	Total £
Employment income	148,200			148,200
Building society interest		7,150		7,150
Dividends			7,556	7,556
	_____	_____	_____	_____
Net income	148,200	7,150	7,556	162,906
Less: PA (Note)	(0)			(0)
	_____	_____	_____	_____
Taxable income	148,200	7,150	7,556	162,906
	_____	_____	_____	_____

Income tax:		
Non-savings – basic rate	39,200 × 20%	7,840
Non-savings – higher rate	109,000 × 40%	43,600
Savings – higher rate	3,300 × 40%	1,320
	_____	
	151,500	
Savings – additional rate	3,850 × 45%	1,733
Dividends – dividend allowance	2,000 × 0%	0
Dividends – additional rate	5,556 × 38.1%	2,117
	_____	
	162,906	
	_____	
Income tax liability		56,610
Less: PAYE		(51,800)
		_____
Income tax payable		4,810
		_____

Tutorial note

The personal allowance is reduced to £Nil as JJ has adjusted net income > £125,140.

Adjusted net income = net income less gross gift aid donations and gross personal pension contributions. As JJ has made gift aid donations, his net income is reduced by the gross donations to give his adjusted net income.

As JJ is an additional rate taxpayer he is not entitled to a savings allowance. All taxpayers are entitled to a dividend allowance of £2,000.

Workings

Extended basic and higher rate bands

	BR band	HR band
	£	£
Basic rate/Higher rate bands	37,700	150,000
Plus: Gift aid (£100 × 12 × 100/80)	1,500	1,500
Extended bands	39,200	151,500

Key answer tips

It is important when using this type of layout to analyse the taxable income into 'non-savings income', 'savings' and 'dividends' as different rates of tax apply to the different sources of income.

Note that:

- The above layout should be possible if the CBA gives five columns to complete the calculation.

- The total lines do not have to be inserted in the real CBA.

- You may find it useful to do the computation on paper first before inputting on screen. This will be especially useful if you are only given three columns to complete in the assessment – where you will only include the total column on screen.

- If the source of income is not specified in the CBA, always assume it is 'non-savings income'.

- It is acceptable to have the total column on the right rather than on the left if you prefer. However, we recommend that the analysis columns are in the fixed order: 'non-savings income', 'savings' and then 'dividends', as this is the order in which they must be taxed through the bands.

28   BILL

Income tax computation – 2021/22

	Non-savings	Savings	Total
	£	£	£
Employment income	54,600		54,600
BSI		3,000	3,000
Net income	54,600	3,000	57,600
Less: PA	(12,570)		(12,570)
Taxable income	42,030	3,000	45,030

Income tax:

Non-savings – basic rate	37,700 × 20%	7,540
Non-savings – higher rate	4,330 × 40%	1,732
Savings – savings allowance	500 × 0%	0
Savings – higher rate	2,500 × 40%	1,000
		─────
	45,030	
	─────	─────
Income tax liability		10,272
Less: Tax credits		
PAYE		(9,340)
		─────
Income tax payable		932
		─────

Tutorial note

As Bill is a higher rate taxpayer he is entitled to a savings allowance of £500.

Key answer tips

It is important when using this type of layout to analyse the taxable income into 'non-savings income', 'savings' and 'dividends' as different rates of tax apply to the different sources of income.

Note that:

- The above layout should be possible provided the CBA gives four columns to complete the calculation.

- The total lines do not have to be inserted in the real CBA.

- You may find it useful to do the computation on paper first before inputting on screen. This will be especially useful if you are only given three columns to complete in the assessment – where you will only include the total column on screen.

- If the source of income is not specified in the CBA, always assume it is 'non-savings income'.

- It is acceptable to have the total column on the right rather than on the left if you prefer. However, we recommend that the analysis columns are in the fixed order: 'non-savings income', 'savings' and then 'dividends', as this is the order in which they must be taxed through the bands.

If you are only provided with 3 columns then this layout will be appropriate

Workings		£
Employment income		54,600
BSI		3,000
		————
Net income		57,600
Less: PA		(12,570)
		————
Taxable income		45,030
		————
Income tax:		
Non-savings – basic rate	37,700 × 20%	7,540
Non-savings – higher rate (£54,600 – £12,570 – £37,700)	4,330 × 40%	1,732
Savings – savings allowance	500 × 0%	0
Savings – higher rate	2,500 × 40%	1,000
	————	
	45,030	
	————	
Income tax liability		10,272
Less: Tax credits – PAYE		(9,340)
		————
Income tax payable		932
		————

Erica

Income tax computation – 2021/22

	Non-savings	Dividends	Total
	£	£	£
Property income (£140,000 – £10,000)	130,000		130,000
Dividends (£15,000 – £6,000)		9,000	9,000
	————	————	————
Net income	130,000	9,000	139,000
Less: PA (W1)	(0)		(0)
	————	————	————
Taxable income	130,000	9,000	139,000
	————	————	————
Income tax:			
Non-savings – basic rate	47,700 (W2) × 20%		9,540
Non-savings – higher rate	82,300 × 40%		32,920
Dividends – dividend allowance	2,000 × 0%		0
Dividends – higher rate	7,000 × 32.5%		2,275
	————		
	139,000		
	————		
Income tax payable			44,735
			————

Workings

(W1) Adjusted personal allowance

	£	£
Personal allowance		12,570
Net income	139,000	
Less: PPC (£8,000 × 100/80)	(10,000)	
	———	
Adjusted net income	129,000	
Adjusted net income > £125,140		
Adjusted PA		0
		———

(W2) Extended basic rate band

	£
Basic rate band	37,700
Plus: PPC (£8,000 × 100/80)	10,000
	———
Extended basic rate band	47,700
	———

Tutorial note

As Erica's adjusted net income exceeds £100,000, her personal allowance must be reduced. Her net income exceeds £125,140 and so the personal allowance would appear to be fully reduced, but adjusted net income must be considered.

Adjusted net income = net income less gross gift aid donations and gross personal pension contributions.

As Erica has made a personal pension contribution, her 'adjusted net income' is lower than her net income but is still more than £125,140 and so no personal allowance is available.

In addition, Erica's basic rate band needs to be extended by the gross pension contribution to determine the appropriate rates of tax to apply.

NATIONAL INSURANCE CONTRIBUTIONS

29   JEREMY

(a)   Jeremy's class 1 NIC is £2,572.

Working	£
(£31,000 − £9,568) × 12%	2,572

Aishah's class 1 NIC is £0.

Hawk Ltd's employer class 1 NIC is £3,150.

Working	£
(£31,000 − £8,840) × 13.8% (Jeremy)	3,058
(£9,510 − £8,840) × 13.8% (Aishah)	92
Total employer class 1 NIC	3,150

Hawk's employer class 1A NIC is £1,104.

Working	
(£800 + £7,200) × 13.8%	£1,104

Tutorial note

No deduction is available for pension contributions or expenses incurred wholly, exclusively and necessarily in the performance of duties when calculating earnings for the purposes of national insurance contributions.

Aishah's cash earnings are below £9,568 so her national insurance contributions are £Nil.

(b)

	True	False
Bo is a self-employed entertainer at children's parties making a profit of £35,000 per year. Bo is required to pay class 1 employee contributions in respect of this profit.		✓

Tutorial note

The statement is false because Bo is self-employed and not an employee.

30   MURRAY

(a)   Joan's class 1 NIC is £1,251.84.

Working	£
(£20,000 – £9,568) × 12%	1,251.84

Murray's class 1 NIC is £6,398.84.

Working	£
(£50,270 – £9,568) × 12%	4,884.24
(£126,000 – £50,270) × 2%	1,514.60
	————
	6,398.84
	————

Lob Roll's employer class 1 NIC is £13,708.16.

Working	£
(£20,000 – £8,840) × 13.8%	1,540.08
(£126,000 – £8,840) × 13.8%	16,168.08
	————
	17,708.16
Less: Employment allowance	(4,000.00)
	————
Employer class 1 NIC	13,708.16
	————

Lob Roll Ltd's class 1A NIC is £1,987.20.

Working	£
£14,400 × 13.8%	1,987.20
	————

Tutorial note

No deduction is available for pension contributions or expenses incurred wholly, exclusively and necessarily in the performance of duties when calculating earnings for the purposes of national insurance contributions.

The employment allowance is available to reduce the employer class 1 national insurance contributions.

(b)

	True	False
Ting has two jobs, one job pays £4,000 per year and the other one pays £9,000. Ting is required to pay class 1 employee contributions.		✓

Tutorial note

The statement is false as Ting is able to use the annual threshold of £9,568 against both employments separately.

31   LUKA

(a)   Luka's liability to class 1 NIC is £5,031.

Working

	£
(£50,270 – £9,568) × 12%	4,884
(£57,600 (£4,800 × 12) – £50,270) × 2%	147
	———
	5,031
	———

Noel's liability to class 1 NIC is £4,612.

Working

	£
(£48,000 (£4,000 × 12) – £9,568) × 12%	4,612

Hound Ltd's employer class 1 NIC is £12,133.

Working

(£57,600 – £8,840) × 13.8%	6,729
(£48,000 – £8,840) × 13.8%	5,404
	———
Employer class 1 NIC	12,133
	———

Hound Ltd's class 1A liability is £1,145.

Working

£8,300 × 13.8%	£1,145

(b)

	True	False
In the tax year 2021/22 Michael earned a gross salary of £37,000. He contributed £3,800 to an occupational pension scheme during the year. Michael's total liability to national insurance contributions for the tax year 2021/22 is £3,291.84 ((£37,000 − £9,568) × 12%).	✓	

Tutorial note

Pension contributions are not deducted when calculating earnings for the purposes of national insurance contributions.

32   LEWIS

(a)   Lewis' class 1 NIC liability is £5,518.84.

Working

	£
(£50,270 − £9,568) × 12%	4,884.24
(£71,000 + £11,000 − £50,270) × 2%	634.60
	————
	5,518.84
	————

Janine's liability to class 1 NIC is £1,851.84.

Working

	£
(£25,000 − £9,568) × 12%	1,851.84

Auto Ltd's employer class 1 NIC is £12,326.16.

Working

(£71,000 + £11,000 − £8,840) × 13.8%	10,096.08
(£25,000 − £8,840) × 13.8%	2,230.08
	————
Employer class 1 NIC	12,326.16
	————

(b)

	True	False
In the tax year 2021/22 Amber earned a salary of £40,000. She was also provided with a company car resulting in a taxable benefit of £3,700.		✓
Amber's total liability to national insurance contributions for the tax year 2021/22 is £4,095.84 ((£40,000 + £3,700 − £9,568) × 12%).		
John has a salary of £30,000 and pays 5% of his salary into an occupational pension scheme. John's employer will pay class 1 national insurance contributions on £30,000.	✓	

Tutorial note

The first statement is false because employees do not pay class 1 contributions in respect of benefits.

The second statement is true because employers pay class 1 contributions on gross earnings.

33 NAOMIE

(a) Naomie's class 1 NIC liability is £3,532.

Working	£
(£39,000 − £9,568) × 12%	3,532

Jeff's class 1 NIC liability is £6,079.

Working	£
(£50,270 − £9,568) × 12%	4,884
(£110,000 − £50,270) × 2%	1,195
	6,079

Pirates Ltd's class 1 NIC is £14,122.

Working	£
(£39,000 − £8,840) × 13.8%	4,162
(£110,000 − £8,840) × 13.8%	13,960
	18,122
Less: Employment allowance	(4,000)
Employer class 1 NIC	14,122

Pirates Ltd's class 1A NIC is £573.

Working

£4,150 (£2,150 + £2,000) × 13.8%   £573

(b)

	True	False
Phillip has a salary of £9,400. He is paid 60p a mile for 6,000 business miles. Phillip has no national insurance liability in the tax year 2021/22.		✓

Tutorial note

As Phillip's gross earnings of £10,300 (£9,400 + (£6,000 × (60p – 45p)) exceed £9,568 this statement is false.

34   REG

(a)   Reg's class 1 NIC liability is £7,078.84.

Working	£
(£50,270 – £9,568) × 12%	4,884.24
(£160,000 – £50,270) × 2%	2,194.60
	7,078.84

Lisa's liability to class 1 NIC is £4,851.84.

Working	£
(£50,000 – £9,568) × 12%	4,851.84

Lleaff Ltd's employer class 1 NIC is £26,540.16.

Working	
(£160,000 – £8,840) × 13.8%	20,860.08
(£50,000 – £8,840) × 13.8%	5,680.08
Employer class 1 NIC	26,540.16

(b)

	True	False
An employer only qualifies for the employment allowance if its class 1 and class 1A national insurance liabilities were less than £100,000 in the previous year.		✓
Contributions by an employee to the employer's occupation pension scheme are deducted from salary when calculating class 1 national insurance contributions.		✓

Tutorial note

The employer's class 1 national insurance contributions for the previous year must be less than £100,000 but the class 1A national insurance contributions are not relevant for this limit.

Pension contributions are not deducted when calculating earnings for the purposes of national insurance contributions.

35 SALLY

(a) Sally's liability to class 1 NIC is £3,172.

Working

	£
(£36,000 – £9,568) × 12%	3,172

Lance's liability to class 1 NIC is £5,559.

Working

	£
(£50,270 – £9,568) × 12%	4,884
(£84,000 – £50,270) × 2%	675
	─────
	5,559
	─────

Twigg Ltd's employer class 1 NIC is £14,120.

Working

(£36,000 – £8,840) × 13.8%	3,748
(£84,000 – £8,840) × 13.8%	10,372
	─────
Employer class 1 NIC	14,120
	─────

Tutorial note

Pension contributions are not deducted when calculating earnings for the purposes of national insurance contributions

(b)

	True	False
The employment allowance is not available if there is only one employee and the employee is a director.	✓	
An employee pays class 1A national insurance contributions on their taxable benefits.		✓

Tutorial note

The employer, not the employee, pays class 1A national insurance contributions on the employee's taxable benefits.

TAX PLANNING

36   FREYA

(a)   (i)   Contribution of £2,000 towards the capital cost of the car.

The CO_2 emissions of 108g/km are rounded down to 105g/km. The appropriate percentage is therefore 25% (15% + (105 – 55) × 1/5).

Freya's capital contribution will reduce the list price by £2,000. Her taxable benefit will therefore be reduced by £500 (2,000 × 25%).

Freya is a higher rate taxpayer. Her tax liability will therefore fall by £200 (£500 × 40%) per year.

(ii)   Contribution of £600 per year towards the cost of using the car for private purposes.

This contribution will reduce the taxable benefit by £600.

Freya's tax liability will therefore fall by £240 (£600 × 40%).

(iii)   Contribution of £480 per year towards the cost of the private use petrol.

This will not have any effect on Freya's income tax liability because she will not be paying the whole of the cost of the petrol used for private purposes. Unless she pays for all her private fuel she is not entitled to a deduction for any partial contributions made and thus makes no saving on the £480 contribution.

(b)   There is no reduction in Richard's income tax liability as he is a basic rate taxpayer (based on £45,000 less £12,570 PA = £32,430 taxable income). The charity will be able to claim an extra £50 (£200 × 20/80).

37   CHRISTINA

(a)   Income tax cost of the train ticket is £0.

Christina exceeded 10,000 business miles in 2021/22 so the approved mileage allowance rate is 25p mile for extra miles above this.

Christina's taxable amount for the London trip was £100 (500 × (45p – 25p)).

Christina is a higher rate taxpayer. Her tax liability will therefore fall by £40 (£100 × 40%) if she had used the train.

(b)   There would be no additional benefit if Russell had lived in the flat as the cost was less than £75,000.

The additional benefit on the house is £1,700 ((£160,000 – £75,000) × 2%).

The income tax saving is therefore £680 (£1,700 × 40%).

Tutorial note

The fact that more than six years have passed between the employer buying the flat and Russell moving in, is not relevant for working out whether the additional benefit applies. If the original cost had exceeded £75,000, the market value would then be used in the additional benefit calculation.

(c)   Bodgan's taxable income is £34,430 (£40,000 + £7,000 – £12,570) and so he is a basic rate taxpayer.

The dividends would have been exempt from tax if held in the individual savings account.

Therefore, the income tax saved is the tax due on the dividends of £375 (£5,000 × 7.5%).

Tutorial note

Income tax is only saved on £5,000 of the dividends as £2,000 would already be taxed at 0% due to the dividend allowance.

(d)   Diane's existing gross personal pension contributions are £7,500 (£500 × 12 × 100/80).

Diane's taxable income is £48,430 (£60,000 + £1,000 – £12,570) which must fall within the basic rate band for the £1,000 savings allowance to be available. This means an additional gross contribution is required of £3,230 (£48,430 – £7,500 – £37,700).

The net contribution required is then £2,584 (80% × £3,230).

38 MITCHELL

(a)

Proposed change	Increase	Decrease	No change
Mitchell contributes a further £1,500 towards the capital cost of the car.			✓
Mitchell has £185 of accessories added to the car on 6 April 2021.	✓		
A car is provided to the same specification but registered on 1 January 2021.		✓	
A car is provided to the same specification but the RDE2 standards are met.		✓	

Workings

(i)   A contribution towards the capital cost of the car, up to a maximum of £5,000, decreases the list price to use in the calculation of the benefit. Mitchell's existing capital contribution exceeds the maximum and so there is no further reduction for the £1,500 contribution.

(ii) The cost of accessories added to the car after it was first provided will be added to the list price if they cost £100 or more.

Therefore the £185 of accessories will increase the benefit and so the income tax.

(iii) If the car had been registered after 6 April 2020, it would not suffer the additional 1% for cars registered before this date.

This will reduce the benefit and so Mitchell's income tax.

(iv) If the car meets the RDE2 standards, it would not suffer the additional 4% for diesel cars not meeting these standards.

This will reduce the benefit and so Mitchell's income tax.

(b)   The pension contribution reduces Sandra's employment income to £149,500, saving £200 (£500 × 40%) income tax on the salary.

The pension contribution reduces Sandra's total income to £150,000, meaning she would no longer be an additional rate taxpayer and would have a savings allowance of £500. This saves income tax on the bank interest of £225 (£500 × 45%) as this is now taxed at 0% rather than 45%.

39   MADELINE

(a)   The approved mileage payments for 20,000 business miles are £7,000 ((10,000 × 45p) + (10,000 × 25p)).

This is the maximum Madeline can receive to pay no income tax, and so the employer's flat rate would be £7,000/20,000 = 35p.

(b)   There is no benefit on the provision of the work gym, so Tanya's employment income decreases by the existing gym subscription of £1,000.

The decrease in income means more of the personal allowance is available of half this amount £500 (£1,000/2).

Tutorial note

For income falling between £100,000 and £125,140, the personal allowance is reduced by £1 for every £2 of income. So a reduction of income of £1,000 means an increase in personal allowance of half of this.

The overall result is that income tax is effectively saved at rate of 60% (£600). This is a saving of £400 in respect of the reduction income itself (£1,000 × 40%) and £200 in respect of the increase in personal allowance (£500 × 40%).

(c)   The petrol car with CO_2 emissions of 121g/km has an appropriate percentage for the car benefit of 28% (being registered after 6 April 2020). This means for a benefit of £8,960 the list price must be £32,000 (£8,960/28%)

The hybrid car has an appropriate percentage of 7% and so the benefit would be £2,240 (£32,000 × 7%).

Therefore, the income tax saved is the tax on the difference i.e. £3,024 (45% × (£8,960 − 2,240)).

Tutorial note

There are several methods which could be used to find the tax saving. One alternative method of calculating the benefit on the hybrid car avoids calculating the list price. Instead the hybrid benefit = 7%/28% × £8,960 = £2,240. This calculation is then used to find the difference in benefit, and the saving in tax as above.

(d)   The maximum investment in the ISA is £20,000, so only dividends on the remaining £80,000 are taxable i.e. £80,000 × 5% = £4,000. The dividend allowance means dividends of £2,000 are taxed at 0%.

Income tax on the dividends is £762 (£2,000 × 38.1%).

40 ANITA

(a)

Proposed change	Increase	Decrease	No change
Anita stops using the van personally except for travel to work.		✓	
Anita makes a £50 per month contribution towards private use of the van.		✓	
Anita made a capital contribution of £2,000 towards the purchase of the van.			✓
The van is changed for a zero emissions model.		✓	
The van is changed for a model with CO_2 emissions of 189g/km.			✓
The company pays for all fuel used by the van.	✓		

(i) Use of a van only for travel to work is not private use for the purpose of a benefit, so no benefit would arise if Anita stops using the van for coaching.

(ii) A monthly contribution towards private use reduces the van benefit.

(iii) A capital contribution does not reduce the van benefit as this is a flat rate and not based on list price.

(iv) A zero emissions van has a £0 benefit.

(v) For any other level of emissions, the van benefit does not change, so higher emissions do not mean a higher benefit amount.

(vi) A van fuel benefit arises if the employer pays for private fuel.

(b) The gross donation would be £10,000 (£8,000 × 100/80). This would extend Frank's basis rate band and increase the higher rate limit so that extra dividends of £10,000 are taxed at 7.5% rather than at 38.1%.

Frank's income tax saving is £3,060 (£10,000 × (38.1% − 7.5%))

Tutorial note

The extension of the basic rate band means a further £10,000 is taxed at 7.5% rather than 32.5%. The increase of the higher rate limit means a further £10,000 is taxed at 32.5% rather than 38.1%. So the amount of dividends taxed at 32.5% remains the same (£112,300). The tax saving is the difference between the additional and basic rates for dividends applied to the gross contribution.

41   TIM

(a)   Tim could receive 10 pence per mile in total for his two passengers.

The daily allowance must decrease by £7.

Tutorial note

The approved mileage allowance is 5p per mile per passenger i.e. 10p in total for the two passengers.

Incidental overnight expenses are exempt up to £5 per night in the UK. Otherwise the full amount, not just the excess, is taxable.

(b)   The taxable benefit on the use of the TV in the tax year 2020/21 is £400 (£2,000 × 20%).

The taxable benefit on the gift of the TV is the higher of:

(i)   the market value at the date of the gift (£1,300), and

(ii)   the market value at the date when first provided to an employee less the taxable benefits charged £1,600 (£2,000 – £400)

less Ian's contribution to the gift.

Ian has to pay £1,600 for the TV to avoid an income tax charge.

(c)   The investment is within the ISA limit and so no tax would arise on the interest or dividends.

Without use of an ISA, the income tax on the building society interest is £90, being 45% on the interest of £200 (£10,000 × 2%).

There is no income tax on the dividends of £700 (£10,000 × 7%) as this is within Yogi's dividend allowance of £2,000.

Yogi's income tax saving from using ISAs is £90.

Tutorial note

An additional rate taxpayer does not have a savings allowance.

All taxpayers have a dividend allowance.

(d)   The full cost of the party of £400 is taxable because the amount exceeds £150 per head. Although the savings allowance means the interest is taxed at 0%, the interest is still part of Aoife's income.

Aoife's income is therefore £105,600 (£105,000 + £400 + £200). To preserve the full personal allowance her adjusted net income needs to be reduced by £5,600 to £100,000. Aoife should make a payment to charity of £4,480 (£5,600 × 80%).

42   **PHILIP**

(a)

Proposed change	Increase	Decrease	No change
Philip decreases his contribution to his personal pension scheme.	✓		
An extension is built to the house in May 2021.			✓
Philip pays rent of £100 per week to live in the house.		✓	
Philip had instead invested the £20,000 cash in a five-year building society account (not an individual savings account) on which he received interest of £1,000 in the tax year 2021/22.	✓		

(i)   Decreasing his contribution, decreases the tax relief due to the extension of Philip's basic rate band.

(ii)   The additional benefit is calculated using the cost of the house including an improvement prior to 6 April 2021. The extension in May 2021 does not increase the benefit in the tax year 2021/22 but will increase it in future years.

(iii)   The accommodation benefit is reduced by employee contributions.

(iv)   Interest earned in the individual savings account was exempt from tax. Philip is a higher rate taxpayer and so has a savings allowance of £500. The remaining £500 of interest from the five-year building society account is taxable.

Tutorial note

A decrease in the employer's pension contribution would have had no effect on Roger's income tax liability as this is a taxable benefit.

(b)   The relocation payment should be reduced by £2,000, as up to £8,000 relocation expenses met by the employer are tax-free.

The increase in the amount of annual interest that Roger should pay is £150. The loan benefit is charged at 2% (the official rate of interest). Roger already pays 1.25% interest, and so a further 0.75% interest payment is required to avoid a tax liability i.e. £20,000 × 0.75% = £150 annually.

Roger's charitable donation is £2,300 (1% of £230,000). The gross donation is £2,875 (£2,300 × 100/80). Roger is an additional rate tax pay so the donation saves tax at 25% (45% – 20%). The income tax saving is £719 (£2,875 × 25%).

CAPITAL GAINS TAX PRINCIPLES

43   TAREQ

(a)

	Actual proceeds used	Deemed proceeds used	No gain no loss basis
Sister gives an asset to her brother		✓	
Civil partner gives an asset to civil partner			✓
Tareq sells an asset to his friend for £38,000. He later discovers the asset is worth £45,000.	✓		

Tutorial note

'Deemed proceeds used' is the term used by the AAT in the past.

*The term means that the **market value of the asset** will be used instead of actual sale proceeds as the starting point of the capital gain computation.*

Market value must be used where there is:

- *a disposal to a connected person (except for inter spouse and civil partnership transfers)*

- *a gift to any person*

- *sales at an undervaluation to anyone (except for inter spouse and civil partnership transfers).*

A sale at undervaluation is where an asset is deliberately/knowingly sold for less than the market value.

A bad bargain (i.e. accidentally selling for less than the asset is worth) will not be caught by special rules and the actual sale proceeds received would be used in this case. A friend is not classed as a connected person for the purposes of this legislation.

Inter spouse and civil partnership transfers are always treated as no gain/no loss transactions.

(b)

Asset	Sale proceeds	Cost	Gain/loss/ exempt	£
1	£5,000	£4,000	Exempt	0
2	£10,000	£7,000	Gain	3,000
3	£9,000	£3,000	Gain	5,000
4	£4,000	£9,000	Loss	3,000

Working

Asset 1: Proceeds and costs are both < £6,000.

Asset 2: No special rules apply, as proceeds and cost are both > £6,000.

Asset 3: Gain is the lower of (£9,000 – £3,000) = £6,000, or 5/3 × (£9,000 – £6,000) = £5,000.

Asset 4: Deemed proceeds of £6,000 must be used.

Tutorial note

The chattel marginal gain rules apply when the proceeds > £6,000 and the cost < £6,000.

The gain is taken to be the lower of

(i)   The gain calculated as normal

(ii)   5/3 × (Gross proceeds – £6,000)

Special loss rules apply when proceeds < £6,000 and the cost > £6,000.

The allowable loss is calculated assuming gross sale proceeds of £6,000.

(c)   The answer is £4,286.

Working

Cost (part disposal)
(£10,000/£10,000 + £25,000) × £15,000   £4,286
                                                                       ‾‾‾‾‾‾‾

Tutorial note

The cost of the chairs sold must be found by applying the part disposal formula to the cost:

Cost × A/A + B

Where   A = gross sales proceeds, and
B = market value of the part of the asset kept.

44   SAMANTHA

(a)

	Actual proceeds used	Deemed proceeds used	No gain no loss basis
Samantha sells an asset to her colleague for £8,000. She then discovers that it was worth £10,000	✓		
Neil sells an asset to his wife for £10,000 when the market value is £14,000			✓
Selim gives an asset to his friend.		✓	

Tutorial note

*'Deemed proceeds used' is the term used by the AAT in the past. The term means that the **market value of the asset** will be used instead of actual sale proceeds as the starting point of the capital gain computation. Market value must be used where there is:*

*   *a disposal to a connected person (except for inter spouse and civil partnership transfers)*

*   *a gift to any person*

*   *a sale at an undervaluation to anyone (except for inter spouse and civil partnership transfers).*

A sale at undervaluation is where an asset is deliberately/knowingly sold for less than the market value.

A bad bargain (i.e. accidentally selling for less than the asset is worth) will not be caught by special rules and the actual sale proceeds received would be used in this case.

Inter spouse and civil partnership transfers are always treated as no gain/no loss transactions.

(b)

		£
A racehorse bought for £4,000 and sold for £7,500	exempt	0
A necklace bought for £5,900 plus £200 of auction costs, and given away when its market value was £8,000	gain	1,900
An antique vase bought for £3,000 and sold for £8,200	gain	3,667
A painting bought for £3,000 and sold for £5,900	exempt	0

Workings

Gain on necklace = £8,000 – £5,900 – £200 = £1,900

Gain on vase is the lower of (£8,200 – £3,000) = £5,200, or 5/3 × (£8,200 – £6,000) = £3,667

Tutorial note

Marginal gain rules only apply when a non-wasting chattel is disposed of and the proceeds are > £6,000 and the cost < £6,000. In this question this only applies to the vase.

The racehorse is a wasting chattel and exempt.

The necklace costs more than £6,000 and has disposal proceeds of more than £6,000.

The painting is exempt as the cost and proceeds are both below £6,000.

Shares are not chattels.

(c)   The answer is £202,000.

Working

	£
Proceeds	400,000
Less: Cost	(155,000)
Conservatory	(15,000)
Extension	(28,000)
Chargeable gain	202,000

45   VICTORIA

(a)

	True	False
Victoria and her cousin Olive are connected persons for capital gains purposes.		✓
A gift from Janet to her husband Mike cannot give rise to a gain or a loss.	✓	
If an asset is destroyed by flooding and insurance proceeds are received this is a chargeable disposal.	✓	

Tutorial note

Cousins do not meet the definition of connected persons.

A gift between wife and husband is made at nil gain nil loss.

The destruction of an asset is a disposal with the insurance received as the proceeds figure.

(b)

	Gain £
Jay bought a building for £70,000. He spent £10,000 on repairs to the building and sold it for £120,000.	50,000
Carli bought an asset for £30,000, selling it for £50,000. She paid auctioneer's commission of 5% when she bought the asset and 4% when she sold the asset.	16,500
Kamilah died on 3 October 2021. She left an antique desk to charity in her will. The desk had cost her £13,000 and was valued for probate at £27,000.	0
Rory owned a set of three paintings. He had bought these for £16,500 in total. He sold one of the paintings for £20,000. The remaining two paintings had a total market value of £36,000.	14,107
James bought a vintage car for £11,500 and sold it for £15,000.	0

Workings

(W1) Building

	£
Proceeds	120,000
Less: Cost	(70,000)
Chargeable gain	50,000

Tutorial note

Repair costs are not capital expenditure and therefore not allowable deductions in the chargeable gains computation.

(W2) Carli's asset

	£
Proceeds	50,000
Less: Selling costs – auctioneers fees (£50,000 × 4%)	(2,000)
	48,000
Less: Cost	(30,000)
Purchase costs – auctioneer's fees (£30,000 × 5%)	(1,500)
Gain	16,500

(W3) Antique desk

The gain is £0.

Tutorial note

Death is not an event giving rise to chargeable disposals.

(W4) Paintings

	£
Proceeds	20,000
Less: Cost £20,000/(£20,000 + £36,000) × £16,500	(5,893)
Chargeable gain	14,107

Tutorial note

The cost of the one painting sold from a set of three must be found by applying the part disposal formula to the cost:

Cost × A/A + B

Where   A = gross sales proceeds (i.e. before selling expenses)
and   B = market value of the part of the asset kept

(W5) Car

A car is exempt, even if it is a vintage car.

46 ESHE

(a)

	True	False
A chargeable gain arises on the gift to a connected person of a necklace costing £8,000 which has increased in value.	✓	
No gain or loss arises if insurance proceeds are received for a painting destroyed in a fire.		✓
A sale to a friend at an intended discount uses the market value for deemed proceeds in the gains calculation.	✓	

Tutorial note

Chargeable gains arise on the following disposals where the proceeds are deemed to be market value:

- *a disposal to a connected person (except for inter spouse and civil partnership transfers)*

- *a gift to any person*

- *a sale at an undervaluation to anyone (except for inter spouse and civil partnership transfers).*

A sale at undervaluation is where an asset is deliberately/knowingly sold for less than the market value.

A bad bargain (i.e. accidentally selling for less than the asset is worth) would not be caught by special rules and the actual sale proceeds received would then be used. A friend is not classed as a connected person for the purposes of this legislation.

The destruction of an asset is a disposal with the insurance received as the proceeds figure.

(b)

	Gain £
Eshe	
Eshe sold a necklace worth £50,000 to her sister for £40,000. The necklace had cost Eshe £31,400 in June 2009.	18,600
Eshe gave a painting to her wife's brother. The painting cost £5,700 and was worth £9,000 at the time of the gift.	3,300
Eshe sold an antique table which had cost £8,000 to her cousin for £11,000. This was the price that an antique dealer had offered to Eshe earlier in the year. Later Eshe discovered its value was in fact £12,000.	3,000
Alvin	
Alvin bought a 10 acre field in May 2010 for £40,000. In June 2021 he sold 4 acres for £83,000 net of £2,000 selling expenses. The remaining 6 acres were valued at £110,000.	65,564
In December 2021 Alvin sold the remaining 6 acres of land for £118,000 which was the gross proceeds before incurring £1,500 selling expenses.	93,936

Workings

Eshe

	£	£
Necklace		
Market value	50,000	
Less: Cost	(31,400)	
	———	
Chargeable gain		18,600
Painting		
Gain lower of:		
Proceeds	9,000	
Less: Cost	(5,700)	
	———	
	3,300	
And 5/3 × (£9,000 – £6,000)	5,000	
Chargeable gain		3,300
Table		
Proceeds	11,000	
Less: Cost	(8,000)	
	———	
Chargeable gain		3,000

Tutorial note

The disposal of the necklace is to a connected person and so market value is automatically substituted for proceeds. Market value is also used as proceeds for disposal of the painting because it is a gift (see above).

Eshe is not connected to her cousin so market value would only be substituted if this was a gift or a deliberate sale at undervalue. This is not the case here so the actual proceeds of £11,000 are used.

Alvin

Disposal in June 2021

	£
Proceeds (£83,000 + £2,000)	85,000
Less: Selling expenses	(2,000)
	———
Net sales proceeds	83,000
Less: Cost £40,000 × (£85,000/£85,000 + £110,000)	(17,436)
	———
Chargeable gain	65,564
	———

Tutorial note

The cost of the land sold must be found by applying the part disposal formula to the cost:

Cost × A/A + B

Where   A = gross sales proceeds (i.e. before selling expenses)
and   B = market value of the part of the asset kept

Questions involving part disposals of a number of acres of land are popular with examiners. It is important to apportion the cost of the part sold using the formula and NOT the number of acres sold.

The cost of the unsold land will be the remainder of the cost.

Disposal in December 2021

	£
Proceeds	118,000
Less: Selling expenses	(1,500)
Net sales proceeds	116,500
Less: Cost (£40,000 – £17,436)	(22,564)
Chargeable gain	93,936

Tutorial note

In questions where selling costs are involved it is very important to note whether the figure provided is given net, or gross, of sales proceeds.

The figure for the sales proceeds regarding the June 2021 disposal is given net of selling costs whereas those provided for the December 2021 disposal are before deduction of selling costs.

47   SAUL

(a)

	Chargeable	Exempt
A machine used in a business and valued at £10,000	✓	
An individual aged under 18 years old	✓	
A gift of a painting (worth £50,000) to a charity		✓

Tutorial note

Machines are wasting chattels which are usually exempt from capital gains tax but not if used in a business.

There is no age limit in respect of chargeable persons for capital gains tax.

A gift to a charity is exempt.

(b)

Asset	Sale proceeds	Cost		£
1	£5,000	£6,000	exempt	0
2	£8,000	£4,000	gain	3,333
3	£7,000	£6,500	gain	500
4	£5,000	£7,000	loss	1,000

Workings for gains and losses:

Asset 2

Gain is the lower of

£4,000 (£8,000 – £4,000) and

$5/3 \times$ (£8,000 – £6,000) = £3,333

Asset 4

Loss is restricted to £1,000 (£6,000 – £7,000)

Tutorial note

Asset 1 cost exactly £6,000 and the proceeds are < £6,000.

The asset is therefore exempt as both the cost and sale proceeds are 'less than or equal to' £6,000.

Asset 4 sales proceeds are < £6,000 but the cost is > £6,000 so the sales proceeds are deemed to be £6,000.

(c) The answer is £60,000.

	£
Proceeds	300,000
Less: Cost	(180,000)
Enhancement expenditure	(60,000)
	————
Chargeable gain	60,000
	————

Tutorial note

Repair costs are not capital expenditure and therefore not allowable deductions in the chargeable gains computation.

48   MARTOK

(a)

	Chargeable	Exempt
An antique clock valued at £20,000		✓
An individual who has no taxable income	✓	
The sale of part of a plot of land	✓	

Tutorial note

Despite being an antique, the clock is treated as machinery and so an exempt wasting asset.

An individual is a chargeable person for capital gains tax, even if they have no taxable income.

A chargeable disposal does not have to involve the sale of the entire asset.

(b)

	Select one option	£
A bravery medal Martok inherited from his father, who had been awarded the medal. The medal was worth £6,400 when Martok inherited it. He sold it for £8,000.	exempt	0
A painting which Martok had bought for £13,000 and sold for £4,000.	loss	7,000
Antique violin sold for £150,000. Martok incurred auctioneer's fees of 1% on this amount. The violin had cost £120,000.	gain	28,500
A ring inherited from his mother which she had bought for £2,000. Its value on inheritance was £8,000 and it was sold for £14,000.	gain	6,000
Shares held in an ISA bought for £5,000 and sold for £35,000.	exempt	0

Workings for gains and losses:

Painting

Loss is restricted to £7,000 (£6,000 – £13,000).

Violin

	£
Proceeds	150,000
Less: Auctioneer's fees (£150,000 × 1%)	(1,500)
Net sales proceeds	148,500
Less: Cost	(120,000)
Chargeable gain	28,500

Ring

Gain is £6,000 (£14,000 – £8,000).

Tutorial note

A decoration for valour acquired other than by purchase (i.e. inherited) is specifically an exempt asset for capital gains tax purposes.

The cost of the ring for Martok's disposal is the value when inherited from his mother, not the initial cost to her.

Although shares are not exempt as chattels, shares held in an ISA are exempt from capital gains tax when sold.

(c)   **Disposal of plot of land**

	£
Proceeds (£68,600 × 100/98)	70,000
Less: Solicitor's fees (£70,000 × 2%)	(1,400)
Net sales proceeds	68,600
Less: Cost £80,000 × (£70,000/£70,000 + £40,000)	(50,909)
Chargeable gain	17,691

Tutorial note

The cost of the land sold must be found by applying the part disposal formula to the cost:

Cost × A/A + B

Where A = gross sales proceeds (i.e. before selling expenses)
and B = market value of the part of the asset kept

Questions involving part disposals of a number of acres of land are popular with examiners. It is important to apportion the cost of the part sold using the formula and NOT the number of acres sold.

The cost of the unsold land will be the remainder of the cost.

49 BARNEY

(a)

	True	False
The death of a taxpayer does not give rise to chargeable disposals.	✓	
Market value is used for the proceeds on disposal of a chargeable asset between civil partners.		✓
A brother and a sister are connected persons for capital gains tax purposes.	✓	

Tutorial note

Death is not an event giving rise to chargeable disposals.

A gift between wife and husband is made at nil gain nil loss i.e. the proceeds are deemed to be the same as cost, not market value.

Siblings are connected persons for capital gains tax purposes.

(b)

	Gain £
Barney gave his daughter cash of £25,000.	0
A statue owned by Barney was destroyed in a storm. Barney received insurance proceeds of £50,000. He had bought the statue for £23,000 in January 2003.	27,000
Barney sold antique furniture to his son for £20,000. The market value was £25,000 but Barney thought the sale to his son was easier than advertising this online. Barney's son paid £200 to transport the furniture from Barney's house. The furniture had cost Barney £19,000 in 2012 and he had paid £500 for expert polishing of the furniture in 2015.	6,000
Barney sold a vase for £3,200 which had cost £2,000.	0
Barney sold the remaining two acres of a plot of land for £100,000. He had bought five acres for £40,000 in 2003 but sold three acres in 2017 for £90,000. At the time of the 2017 sale, the remaining two acres were worth £50,000.	84,714

Workings for gains and losses:

Statue

	£
Proceeds	50,000
Less: Cost	(23,000)
Chargeable gain	27,000

Furniture

	£
Proceeds (market value)	25,000
Less: Cost	(19,000)
Chargeable gain	6,000

Land

	£
Proceeds	100,000
Less: Cost £40,000 – £40,000 × (£90,000/£90,000 + £50,000)	(14,286)
Chargeable gain	85,714

Tutorial note

Cash is not a chargeable asset for capital gains tax purposes.

The destruction of an asset is a disposal with the insurance received as the proceeds figure.

The sale of an asset at undervalue to a connected person gives rise to a gain using market value for the proceeds.

Polishing costs are not capital expenditure and therefore not allowable deductions in the chargeable gains computation

The vase is a chattel with proceeds and cost both < £6,000 and so no gain arises.

In 2017, there was a part disposal of land. The cost of the land sold then would have been found by applying the part disposal formula to the cost:

Cost × A/A + B

Where   A = gross sales proceeds (i.e. before selling expenses)
and   B = market value of the part of the asset kept

The cost of the unsold land is the remainder of the cost and so this the cost that should be used in the gains calculation for the tax year 2021/22.

CAPITAL GAINS TAX: DISPOSALS OF SHARES

50   STRINGER LTD

Chargeable gain calculation – 2021/22	£
Proceeds (5,000 × £10)	50,000
Less: Cost (W)	(20,833)
Chargeable gain	29,167

Working: Share pool

		Number	Cost £
July 2012	Purchase (8,000 × £8)	8,000	64,000
March 2013	Purchase (4,000 × £9)	4,000	36,000
		12,000	100,000
July 2015	Sale (£100,000 × 3,000/12,000)	(3,000)	(25,000)
		9,000	75,000
May 2019	Bonus issue (1 for 1)	9,000	0
		18,000	75,000
Feb 2022	Sale (£75,000 × 5,000/18,000)	(5,000)	(20,833)
Balance c/f		13,000	54,167

Key answer tips

Remember you are only being asked to calculate the gain on the February 2022 disposal. The July 2015 disposal is only important for the pool calculation. The sales proceeds at this date are irrelevant here.

The disposal in July 2015 will reduce the balance of the pool for the later disposal so calculate the cost of the share sold in the usual way then add down to give the balance to carry forward.

You are also asked for the chargeable gain, not the taxable gain; therefore do not waste time deducting the annual exempt amount.

51 LULU LTD

Chargeable gain calculation

	£
Proceeds (8,000 × £7)	56,000
Less: Cost (W)	(29,538)
Chargeable gain	**26,462**

Working: Share pool

		Number	Cost £
Oct 2010	Purchase (6,000 × £3)	6,000	18,000
May 2011	Purchase (6,000 × £5)	6,000	30,000
		12,000	48,000
June 2012	Bonus 1 for 12	1,000	0
		13,000	48,000
April 2016	Sale (£48,000 × 3,000/13,000)	(3,000)	(11,077)
		10,000	36,923
Jan 2022	Sale (£36,923 × 8,000/10,000)	(8,000)	(29,538)
Balance c/f		2,000	7,385

Key answer tips

Remember you are only being asked to calculate the gain on the January 2022 disposal. The April 2016 disposal is only important for the pool calculation. The sales proceeds at this date are irrelevant here.

The disposal in April 2016 will reduce the balance of the pool for the later disposal so calculate the cost of the share sold in the usual way then add down to give the balance to carry forward.

You are also asked for the chargeable gain, not the taxable gain; therefore do not waste time deducting the annual exempt amount.

52 GILBERT LTD

Chargeable gain calculation

			£
1	On 1,200 shares matched with the 15 September 2021 purchase		
	Proceeds 1,200/8,000 × £65,000		9,750
	Less: Cost		(9,600)
			———
	Chargeable gain		150
			———
2	On 1,000 shares matched with the 18 September 2021 purchase		
	Proceeds 1,000/8,000 × £65,000		8,125
	Less: Cost		(10,000)
			———
	Loss		(1,875)
			———
3	On 5,800 shares matched with the pool		
	Proceeds (£65,000 – £9,750 – £8,125)		47,125
	Less: Cost (W)		(23,200)
			———
	Chargeable gain		23,925
			———
	Total gain (£23,925 + £150 – £1,875)		22,200
			———

Working: Share pool

		Number	Cost £
May 2009	Purchase (8,000 × £6)	8,000	48,000
June 2013	Bonus 1 for 2	4,000	0
		———	———
		12,000	48,000
Sept 2021	Sale (£48,000 × 5,800/12,000)	(5,800)	(23,200)
		———	———
	Balance c/f	6,200	24,800
		———	———

Tutorial note

In relation to individuals, we match shares disposed of in the following order:

- *first, with shares acquired on the same day as the disposal*
- *second, with shares acquired within the following 30 days (using the earliest acquisition first, i.e. on a FIFO basis)*
- *third, with the share pool (all the shares bought before the date of disposal).*

In this case there are 1,200 shares purchased on 15 September 2021 and 1,000 purchased on 18 September 2021, both of which are within 30 days after the disposal on 7 September 2021. Hence 1,200 of the shares sold on 7 September are matched with the purchase on 15 September, and then 1,000 shares are matched with the purchase on 18 September.

The remaining 5,800 shares sold are matched with the share pool.

53   BELLA

Chargeable gain calculation

1   On 1,000 shares matched with the 17 May 2021 purchase

	£
Proceeds (1,000 × £11)	11,000
Less: Cost (1,000 × £10)	(10,000)
Chargeable gain	1,000

2   On pool shares

	£
Proceeds (8,000 × £11)	88,000
Less: Cost (W)	(46,222)
Chargeable gain	41,778

Total gain (£1,000 + £41,778)	42,778

Working: Share pool

		Number	Cost £
Sept 2012	Purchase (20,000 × £6)	20,000	120,000
July 2014	Sale (£120,000 × 4,000/20,000)	(4,000)	(24,000)
		16,000	96,000
June 2016	Rights issue 1 for 8 (2,000 × £4)	2,000	8,000
		18,000	104,000
May 2021	Sale (£104,000 × 8,000/18,000)	(8,000)	(46,222)
Balance c/f		10,000	57,778

Tutorial note

In relation to individuals, we match shares disposed of in the following order:

- *first, with shares acquired on the same day as the disposal*

- *second, with shares acquired within the following 30 days (using the earliest acquisition first, i.e. on a FIFO basis)*

- *third, with the share pool (all the shares bought before the date of disposal).*

In this case there are 1,000 shares purchased on 17 May 2021 which is within 30 days after the disposal on 14 May 2021. Hence 1,000 of the shares sold on 14 May are matched with the purchase on 17 May.

The remaining 8,000 shares sold are matched with the share pool.

54   BAJOR PLC

Chargeable gain calculation

	£
Proceeds	17,500
Less: Cost (W)	(9,035)
	————
Chargeable gain	8,465
	————

Working: Share pool

		Number	Cost £
Feb 2010	Purchase	2,000	7,560
July 2012	Bonus 1 for 10	200	0
Dec 2014	Purchase	500	2,800
		————	————
		2,700	10,360
Apr 2016	Rights issue (1 for 5) at £2.50	540	1,350
		————	————
		3,240	11,710
Mar 2022	Sale (£11,710 × 2,500/3,240)	(2,500)	(9,035)
		————	————
Balance c/f		740	2,675
		————	————

55 ASPEN LTD

Chargeable gain calculation

		£
1	On 200 shares matched with the 18 June 2021 purchase	
	Proceeds (200 × £6)	1,200
	Less: Cost (200 × £5.5)	(1,100)
	Chargeable gain	100
2	On 400 shares matched with the 25 June 2021 purchase	
	Proceeds (400 × £6)	2,400
	Less: Cost (400 × £7)	(2,800)
	Loss	(400)
3	On 1,400 shares matched with the pool	
	Proceeds (1,400 × £6)	8,400
	Less: Cost (W)	(4,667)
	Chargeable gain	3,733
	Total gain (£3,733 + £100 – £400)	3,433

Working: Share pool

		Number	Cost £
Nov 2016	Purchase (4,000 × £5)	4,000	20,000
July 2018	Bonus 1 for 2	2,000	0
		6,000	20,000
June 2021	Sale (£20,000 × 1,400/6,000)	(1,400)	(4,667)
Balance c/f		4,600	15,333

Tutorial note

In relation to individuals, we match shares disposed of in the following order:

- *first, with shares acquired on the same day as the disposal*
- *second, with shares acquired within the following 30 days (using the earliest acquisition first, i.e. on a FIFO basis)*
- *third, with the share pool (all the shares bought before the date of disposal).*

Kerry purchased 200 shares on the date of disposal so we match with these first. She then purchased 400 shares on 25 June 2021, which is within 30 days after the disposal on 18 June 2021. Hence 400 of the shares sold on 18 June are matched with the purchase on 25 June.

The remaining 1,400 shares sold are matched with the share pool.

56   CHERY LTD

Chargeable gain calculation

	£
Proceeds	91,000
Less: Cost (W)	(56,000)
Chargeable gain	35,000

Working: Share pool

		Number	Cost £
Aug 2013	Purchase (10,000 × £8)	10,000	80,000
Sep 2015	Rights issue (1 for 2) at £6	5,000	30,000
		15,000	110,000
Feb 2019	Sale (£110,000 × 3,000/15,000)	(3,000)	(22,000)
		12,000	88,000
Jan 2022	Purchase (2,000 × £12)	2,000	24,000
		14,000	112,000
Jan 2022	Sale (£112,000 × 7,000/14,000)	(7,000)	(56,000)
Balance c/f		7,000	56,000

Key answer tips

Remember you are only being asked to calculate the gain on the January 2022 disposal. The February 2019 disposal is only important for the pool calculation. The sales proceeds at this date are irrelevant here.

The disposal in February 2019 will reduce the balance of the pool for the later disposal so calculate the cost of the share sold in the usual way then add down to give the balance to carry forward.

There is a purchase of shares in January 2022 as well as a sale but the purchase is made before the sale and is added to the pool as usual. The matching rules only require purchases acquired within the 30 days *following* a sale to be considered separately.

CAPITAL GAINS TAX: RELIEFS AND EXEMPTIONS

57   JOANNA

(a)

	True	False
Capital gains are taxed at 10% for all taxpayers.		✓
If a taxpayer does not use his or her annual exempt amount in the tax year 2019/20 they can bring it forward to use in the tax year 2020/21.		✓
The use of brought forward capital losses is made after the annual exempt amount.	✓	
The last nine months of ownership of a main residence are treated as a period of ownership for private residence relief.	✓	

Tutorial note

The rate of capital gains tax depends on the level of the taxable income.

Taxable gains are taxed after taxable income.

Taxable gains falling into the basic rate band are taxed at 10%. Those gains falling into the higher rate band are taxed at 20%.

If a taxpayer does not use their annual exempt amount for capital gains tax purposes, it cannot be carried forward or backwards and it cannot be given away. It is wasted (i.e. lost).

(b)   Paul's taxable gains for the tax year 2021/22 are £14,510 and his brought forward allowable losses to the tax year 2022/23 are £0.

Working

		Taxable gain £
2019/20	Gain	15,000
	Less: Current year loss	(4,180)
	Net gain	10,820
	Less: Annual exempt amount (part)	(10,820)
	Taxable gain	0

		Taxable gain £
2020/21	Gain	24,960
	Less: Current year loss	(1,400)
	Net gain	23,560
	Less: Annual exempt amount	(12,300)
		11,260
	Less: Loss brought forward	(0)
	Taxable gain	11,260
2021/22	Gain	28,940
	Less: Current year loss	(2,130)
		26,810
	Less: Annual exempt amount	(12,300)
		14,510
	Less: Loss brought forward	(0)
	Taxable gain	14,510

Tutorial note

Start with the earliest year given. For each year deduct from the gain, in this order:

–   *current year losses, if any*

–   *annual exempt amount*

–   *brought forward losses.*

(c)   The taxable gain is £5,108 and the capital gains tax is £695.

Working

Capital gains tax payable computation – 2021/22

	£
Gross sale proceeds	25,927
Less: Selling costs (2% × £25,927)	(519)
	———
Net sale proceeds	25,408
Less: Cost	(8,000)
	———
Chargeable gain	17,408
Less: Annual exempt amount	(12,300)
	———
Taxable gain	5,108
	———

Capital gains tax:

£	
3,270 × 10% (W)	327
1,838 × 20%	368
———	
5,108	
———	———
Capital gains tax payable	695
	———

Remaining basic rate band

	£
Basic rate band	37,700
Less: Taxable income (£47,000 – £12,570)	(34,430)
	———
Remaining basic rate band	3,270
	———

Tutorial note

The taxable gain is the chargeable gain after deducting the annual exempt amount.

The taxable income falls below the basic rate band threshold, therefore there is some of the basic rate band remaining to match against the taxable gains.

Taxable gains fall partly into the remaining basic rate band and partly into the higher rate band. The capital gains tax liability is therefore calculated in two parts at 10% and 20%.

58 KEVIN

(a) Kevin has made the following statements. Advise Kevin whether they are true or false.

Tick the appropriate box for each statement.

	True	False
Unused personal allowance can be deducted from taxable gains.		✓
A taxpayer can live away from their main residence for any reason for up to five years and benefit from full private residence relief.		✓
Current year capital losses are restricted to protect the annual exempt amount.		✓
A capital loss made on a disposal to a connected person can only be deducted from gains on disposals to the same connected person.	✓	

Tutorial note

Only the annual exempt amount can be deducted from chargeable gains, the personal allowance can only be deducted from income.

The maximum period the taxpayer can be away from their main residence for any reason (other than periods working away) is three years and they must occupy the property at some point both before and after the absence.

Current year capital losses are offset before the annual exempt amount and cannot be restricted to preserve it.

(b) The chargeable gain on the sale of the house is £104,125.

Workings

(W1) Total ownership

The house is owned from 1 July 2011 to 30 June 2021 = 10 years or 120 months

(W2) Periods of residence and deemed residence

Occupation and deemed occupation	Mths	Non-occupation	Mths
1 Jul 2011 – 30 Jun 2013	24		
1 Jul 2013 – 30 Jun 2014 (Part of 3 years any reason)	12		
1 Jul 2014 – 30 Jun 2016	24	1 Jul 2016 – 30 Sept 2020	51
1 Oct 2020 – 30 Jun 2021 (Last 9 months)	9		
Total	69		51

(W3) Capital gain on sale of house

	£
Proceeds	285,000
Less: Cost	(40,000)
	245,000
Less: PRR 69/120 × £245,000	(140,875)
Chargeable gain	104,125

Tutorial note

The last nine months of ownership are always deemed occupation even if the taxpayer has another residence by then.

Other deemed residence periods:

(i)   Any period working abroad

(ii)   Up to a total of 4 years working elsewhere in the UK.

(iii)   Up to a total of 3 years for any reason.

These periods must be preceded at some time by actual occupation and followed by actual occupation (except occupation after the absence is not insisted on for (i) and (ii) if the taxpayer cannot return to their residence due to being moved elsewhere to work.)

Esme cannot claim the 'working abroad' period as deemed occupation as she was not working. However, she is always entitled to the last nine months and the period abroad can be covered by 3 years for any reason rule.

The remainder of the 3 years for any reason does not cover the period while living with her boyfriend as she does not reoccupy the property at any time after the period of absence.

(c)   Ruth's taxable gains for the tax year 2021/22 are £5,480 and her brought forward allowable losses to the tax year 2022/23 are £0.

Working

		£
2019/20	Gain	9,340
	Less: Current year loss	(9,340)
	Taxable gain	0
	Loss carried forward (£15,690 – £9,340)	6,350
2020/21	Gain	16,700
	Less: Current year loss	(1,500)
	Net gain	15,200
	Less: Annual exempt amount	(12,300)
		2,900
	Less: Loss brought forward from 2019/20	(2,900)
	Taxable gain	0
	Loss carried forward (£6,350 – £2,900)	3,450
2021/22	Gain	46,900
	Less: Current year loss	(25,670)
		21,230
	Less: Annual exempt amount	(12,300)
		8,930
	Less: Loss brought forward	(3,450)
	Taxable gain	5,480
	Loss carried forward	0

Tutorial note

Start with the earliest year given. For each year deduct from the gain, in the order:

–   *current year losses, if any*

–   *annual exempt amount*

–   *brought forward losses.*

(d)

		£
Gains		31,900
Capital losses		(4,100)
		27,800
Less: Annual exempt amount		(12,300)
Taxable gains		15,500

	£		
	7,200	× 10%	720
(£15,500 – £7,200)	8,300	× 20%	1,660
	15,500		2,380

59 ANGELA

(a)

	True	False
Unused annual exempt amount can be transferred to a spouse or civil partner.		✓
Unused allowable losses are carried forward to be deducted from chargeable gains in future tax years.	✓	
Taxpayers can have several main residences for private residence relief provided they live at least nine months in each one.		✓
Capital gains tax is paid at 20% on gains made by a higher rate taxpayer.	✓	

Tutorial note

The annual exempt amount cannot be transferred to another taxpayer.

Taxpayers can have one main residence at a certain time for private residence relief.

(b) The amount chargeable to capital gains tax (taxable gains) for Mo for the tax year 2021/22 is £0 and his brought forward allowable losses to the tax year 2022/23 are £14,600.

Working

		Taxable gain
		£
2019/20	Gain	25,800
	Less: Current year loss	(14,600)
	Net gain	11,200
	Less: Annual exempt amount (part)	(11,200)
	Taxable gain	0
2020/21	Gain	8,900
	Less: Current year loss	(8,900)
	Taxable gain	0
	Loss carried forward (£23,500 – £8,900)	14,600
2021/22	Gain	6,300
	Less: Current year loss	(0)
		6,300
	Less: Annual exempt amount (part)	(6,300)
	Taxable gain	0
	Losses carried forward	14,600

Tutorial note

Start with the earliest year given. For each year deduct from the gain, in this order:

– *current year losses, if any*

– *annual exempt amount*

– *brought forward losses.*

(c)   The answer is £18,445.

Working

Capital gains tax computation – 2021/22

	£
Sale proceeds	290,000
Less: Cost	(150,000)
Enhancement expenditure	(29,700)
	————
Chargeable gain	110,300
Less: Annual exempt amount	(12,300)
	————
Taxable gains	98,000
	————

Capital gains tax:

	£	
11,555 × 10% (W)		1,156
86,445 × 20%		17,289
————		
98,000		
————		

Capital gains tax payable	18,445
	————

Remaining basic rate band

	£
Basic rate band	37,700
Less: Taxable income	(26,145)
	————
Remaining basic rate band	11,555
	————

Tutorial note

The taxable income falls below the basic rate band threshold, therefore there is some of the basic rate band remaining to match against the taxable gains.

Taxable gains fall partly into the remaining basic rate band and partly into the higher rate band. The capital gains tax liability is therefore calculated in two parts at 10% and 20%.

---

60   LYNNETTE

(a)

	True	False
An additional rate taxpayer does not have an annual exempt amount.		✓
Brought forward capital losses are offset after the annual exempt amount.	✓	
Allowable losses can be transferred to a spouse or civil partner.		✓
Capital gains tax is paid at 38.1% on share gains made by an additional rate taxpayer.		✓

Tutorial note

Each individual has an annual exempt amount regardless of the level of taxable income.

Allowable losses cannot be transferred to another taxpayer.

Capital gains tax is paid at 20% on share gains made by an additional rate taxpayer. The rate of 38.1% is the income tax rate on dividends received by an additional rate taxpayer.

(b)   Lynnette is away from her house for 12 years and never returns.

As she cannot return to her house because of her job, she can claim deemed occupation for 4 years working elsewhere in the UK. However, she cannot have the 3 years for any reason as she does not return to the house.

The last nine months of ownership are always deemed occupation.

Total occupation plus deemed occupation is 12.75 years out of the 20 owned.

	£
Capital gain	360,000
Less: Private residence relief (360,000 × 12.75/20)	(229,500)
Chargeable gain	130,500

(c)   The answer is £560.

Working

Capital gains tax computation – 2021/22

	£
Chargeable gain	17,900
Less: Annual exempt amount	(12,300)
Taxable gains	5,600

Capital gains tax:

	£
5,600 × 10%	560
	——
Capital gains tax payable	560
	——

Remaining basic rate band

	£
Basic rate band	37,700
Less: Taxable income	(24,500)
	——
Remaining basic rate band	13,200
	——

(d) The amount chargeable to capital gains tax (taxable gains) for Candice for the tax year 2021/22 is £0 and her brought forward allowable losses to the tax year 2022/23 are £11,900.

Working

		Taxable gain
		£
2019/20	Gain	4,500
	Less: Current year loss	(4,500)
		——
	Taxable gain	0
		——
	Losses carried forward (£18,300 – £4,500)	13,800
		——
2020/21	Gain	17,400
	Less: Current year loss	(3,200)
		——
		14,200
	Less: Annual exempt amount	(12,300)
		——
		1,900
	Less: Losses brought forward	(1,900)
		——
	Taxable gain	0
		——
	Losses carried forward (£13,800 – £1,900)	11,900
		——
2021/22	Gain	12,900
	Less: Current year loss	(1,200)
		——
		11,700
	Less: Annual exempt amount (part)	(11,700)
		——
	Taxable gain	0
		——
	Losses carried forward	11,900
		——

61   ALYSHA

(a)

	True	False
Current year allowable losses are deducted from current year gains, before the annual exempt amount is deducted.	✓	
The rate of capital gains tax depends on the level of taxable income.	✓	
Married couples and civil partners have one annual exempt amount between them.		✓
Gains made on disposals to a connected person can only be reduced by losses made on disposals to the same connected person.		✓

Tutorial note

Each individual has their own annual exempt amount.

Losses made on disposals to the same connected person can only be offset against gains made on disposals to the same connected person. The gains made can be reduced by allowable losses on any disposals.

(b)   The amount chargeable to capital gains tax (taxable gains) for Tony for the tax year 2021/22 is £1,600 and his brought forward allowable losses to the tax year 2022/23 are £0.

Working

		Taxable gain
		£
2019/20	Gain	53,900
	Less: Current year loss	(24,400)
		29,500
	Less: Annual exempt amount	(12,000)
	Taxable gain	17,500
2020/21	Gain	2,500
	Less: Current year loss	(2,500)
	Taxable gain	0
	Losses carried forward (£19,200 − £2,500)	16,700

		Taxable gain
		£
2021/22	Gain	33,000
	Less: Current year loss	(2,400)
		30,600
	Less: Annual exempt amount	(12,300)
		18,300
	Less: Losses brought forward	(16,700)
	Taxable gain	1,600
	Losses carried forward	0

(c)

	£
Proceeds	52,000
Less: Selling costs – auctioneers fees (£52,000 × 2%)	(1,040)
	50,960
Less: Cost	(35,300)
Purchase costs – legal fees	(250)
Chargeable gain	15,410
Less: Annual exempt amount	(12,300)
Taxable gain	3,110
Capital gains tax (£3,110 × 20%)	622

Tutorial note

Accountant's fees for preparing a capital gains tax computation are not an allowable cost for capital gain purposes.

Capital gains tax is calculated at 20% as Alysha is a higher rate taxpayer.

62   TINEKE

(a)

	True	False
All taxable gains of a basic rate taxpayer are taxed at 10%.		✓
Current year allowable losses must be deducted from current year gains, before any excess losses are carried forward.	✓	
Gains on disposals to connected persons are taxed at the same rates of capital gains tax as gains on disposals to unconnected persons.	✓	
The annual exempt amount is deducted from the capital gains tax for the tax year.		✓

Tutorial note

A basic rate taxpayer pays capital gains tax at 10% on gains that fall within their remaining basic rate band. Gains in excess of this are taxed at 20%.

The annual exempt amount is deducted from chargeable gains, not from capital gains tax.

(b)   The amount chargeable to capital gains tax (taxable gains) for Lissa for the tax year 2021/22 is £7,000 and her brought forward allowable losses to the tax year 2022/23 are £0.

Working

		Taxable gain £
2019/20	Gain	11,400
	Less: Current year loss	(11,400)
		————
	Taxable gain	0
		————
	Losses carried forward (£14,500 – £11,400)	3,100
		————
2020/21	Gain	33,000
	Less: Current year loss	(1,300)
		————
		31,700
	Less: Annual exempt amount	(12,300)
		————
		19,400
	Less: Losses brought forward	(3,100)
		————
	Taxable gain	16,300
		————

		Taxable gain
		£
2021/22	Gain	24,000
	Less: Current year loss	(4,700)
		19,300
	Less: Annual exempt amount	(12,300)
	Taxable gain	7,000
	Losses carried forward	0

(c) **Capital gain on sale of flat**

	£
Proceeds	169,000
Less: Cost	(99,000)
	70,000
Less: PRR 4.75/9 (W) × £70,000	(36,944)
Chargeable gain	33,056

Working

Tineke owned the flat for nine years (1 January 2013 to 31 December 2021).

She is away for two years for work, but this is a period of deemed occupation as she lives in the flat before and after this period of absence.

Tineke did not occupy the flat for the last five years, but the last nine months are included as deemed occupation.

Total occupation and deemed occupation = 1 + 2 + 1 + 0.75 = 4.75 years

Tutorial note

A taxpayer's private residence is exempt for the periods when it is occupied or deemed occupied.

The last nine months of ownership are always deemed occupation even if the taxpayer has another residence by then.

Other deemed residence periods:

(i) *Any period working abroad – this covers Tineke's two years abroad.*

(ii) *Up to a total of 4 years working elsewhere in the UK*

(iii) *Up to a total of 3 years for any reason.*

These periods must be preceded at some time by actual occupation and followed by actual occupation (except occupation after the absence is not insisted on for (i) and (ii) if the taxpayer cannot return to their residence due to being moved elsewhere to work).

This means that the 3 years for any reason cannot be applied to the time Tineke lives with her boyfriend as she does not return to the flat.

(d) The answer is £2,620.

Working

Capital gains tax computation – 2021/22

	£
Chargeable gain	27,000
Less: Annual exempt amount	(12,300)
Taxable gains	14,700

Capital gains tax:

£	
3,200 × 10%	320
11,500 (14,700 – 3,200) × 20%	2,300
Capital gains tax payable	2,620

Remaining basic rate band

	£
Basic rate band	37,700
Less: Taxable income	(34,500)
Remaining basic rate band	3,200

63   KIESWETTER

(a)

	True	False
Private residence relief reduces the amount of gain chargeable on disposal of a main residence.	✓	
The available annual exempt amount is reduced if gains exceed £100,000.		✓
A taxpayer can decide whether to deduct brought forward allowable losses from a gain in a tax year or carry the losses further forward.		✓
Unused annual exempt amount is wasted and cannot be used in other tax years.	✓	

Tutorial note

The annual exempt amount is a fixed amount regardless of level of income.

A brought forward loss must be used against current year gains after deduction of the annual exempt amount. Only amounts that cannot be used can be carried forward.

(b) The amount chargeable to capital gains tax (taxable gains) for Ade for the tax year 2021/22 is £0 and his brought forward allowable losses to the tax year 2022/23 are £1,800.

Working

		Taxable gain
		£
2019/20	Gain	55,000
	Less: Current year loss	(24,500)
		30,500
	Less: Annual exempt amount	(12,000)
	Taxable gain	18,500
2020/21	Gain	3,500
	Less: Current year loss	(3,500)
	Taxable gain	0
	Losses carried forward (£9,600 – £3,500)	6,100
2021/22	Gain	18,600
	Less: Current year loss	(2,000)
		16,600
	Less: Annual exempt amount	(12,300)
		4,300
	Less: Losses brought forward	(4,300)
	Taxable gain	0
	Losses carried forward (£6,100 – £4,300)	1,800

Tutorial note

Start with the earliest year given. For each year deduct from the gain, in this order:

– *current year losses, if any*

– *annual exempt amount*

– *brought forward losses.*

(c) Kieswetter's amount chargeable to capital gains tax is £16,800.

Working

	£
Capital gains for the year	40,300
Less: Capital losses for the year	(4,500)
Net gains	35,800
Less: Annual exempt amount	(12,300)
	23,500
Less: Capital losses brought forward	(6,700)
Taxable gains	16,800

Tutorial note

All current year losses must be set against current year capital gains, even if they waste the annual exempt amount.

Capital losses brought forward are used after the annual exempt amount.

Kieswetter's capital gains tax is £3,360.

Working

Capital gains tax computation – 2021/22

Capital gains tax:

	£
16,800 × 20%	3,360
Capital gains tax payable	3,360

Kieswetter has taxable income exceeding the basis rate band and so the gains are taxable at 20%.

INHERITANCE TAX

64 JANETTE

(a)

	True	False
The annual exemption can be carried forward for one year but cannot be used until the annual exemption for the current year has been used.	✓	
An exempt transfer may give rise to an inheritance tax liability if the donor dies within seven years.		✓
Chargeable lifetime transfers may give rise to two separate liabilities to inheritance tax.	✓	
Taper relief will reduce a transfer of value made more than three but less than seven years prior to the donor's death.		✓
Where the donor of a potentially exempt transfer dies within seven years of making the gift, any inheritance tax due is payable by the donee.	✓	

Tutorial note

The second statement is false because there cannot be an inheritance tax liability where a transfer is exempt. It is a potentially exempt transfer which may give rise to an inheritance tax liability if the donor dies within seven years.

The third statement is true because there may be a charge at the time of the gift and a further charge if the donor dies within seven years.

The fourth statement is false because taper relief reduces the inheritance tax due and not the transfer of value.

(b) (i) Janette has never been married. She does not own a property. The maximum nil rate band available when calculating inheritance tax on her death is £325,000.

Tutorial note

The residence nil rate band is only available in respect of a residence in the death estate.

(ii)   The rate of lifetime inheritance tax charged on a chargeable lifetime transfer (CLT) where the donor pays the tax is 25%.

Tutorial note

If the donor pays the inheritance tax due on a chargeable lifetime transfer, the tax rate is 25%. If the donee pays, the rate is 20%. The inheritance tax rate on death is 40%. The rate of 45% relates to income tax.

(c)

Lifetime gift	CLT	PET	Exempt
£310 from Sharon to her husband.			✓
A house worth £510,000 to a trust.	✓		
£4,000 from Maysoun to her grandson on his wedding day.		✓	

Tutorial note

This first gift would be covered by the spouse exemption.

A gift to a trust is a CLT

The gift is a PET although the marriage exemption of £2,500 would be available in respect of this gift.

65   FLORENCE

(a)

	True	False
The small gifts exemption is £250 per donor per tax year.		✓
No inheritance tax liability can arise in respect of a gift made more than seven years prior to death.		✓
An individual who has always lived in America and is not domiciled in the UK may still be liable to pay inheritance tax in the UK.	✓	
The inheritance tax due in respect of the residue of a death estate is paid by the residuary legatee.		✓
The annual exemption cannot be deducted from the death estate even if there have been no gifts in the year of death.	✓	

Tutorial note

*The first statement is false because the exemption is per **donee** and not per donor.*

The second statement is false because an inheritance tax liability can arise in respect of a chargeable lifetime transfer at any time in a donor's lifetime.

The third statement is true because a person who is not domiciled in the UK may still be subject to UK inheritance tax in respect of assets situated in the UK.

*The fourth statement is false because, although the inheritance tax due in respect of the residue of a death estate is **suffered** by the residuary legatee, it is **paid** by the personal representatives.*

(b) (i) Florence died in 2019. She used her full nil rate band on her death but none of her residence nil rate band. Florence's husband Logan died in 2021. The maximum amount of nil rate band and residence nil rate band that may be available when calculating the inheritance tax on Logan's death is £675,000.

Logan has his own nil rate band available of £325,000, and possibly his residence nil rate band of £175,000 and his wife's residence nil rate band of £175,000, totalling £675,000.

Tutorial note

Logan would have to own a residence and leave this to a direct descendant to benefit from the residence nil rate bands.

(ii) The rate of taper relief that applies to inheritance tax on a gift made in May 2018 if the donor dies in April 2021 is 0%.

The donor did not survive for three years and so no taper relief is available.

(c)

Gift	PET	CLT	Exempt
A statue worth £830,000 from Eric to a national museum.			✓
£10,000 from Janine to her son.	✓		
Gift of cash of £500,000 to a trust.		✓	

Tutorial note

The first gift would be covered by the exemption in respect of gifts to museums and art galleries.

A gift to an individual who is not a spouse or civil partner is a potentially exempt transfer.

A gift to a trust is a chargeable lifetime transfer.

66   ROWENA

	True	False
Lifetime inheritance tax is charged at 25% on a chargeable lifetime transfer where the donor is paying the tax.	✓	
An individual who is domiciled outside the UK is liable to inheritance tax in respect of their worldwide assets.		✓
The annual exemption can be carried forward for one year and must be used before the annual exemption for the current year.		✓
A gift to a political party is an exempt transfer.	✓	
The residence nil rate band is available on a lifetime gift of a residence from mother to son.		✓

Tutorial note

The second statement is false because an individual who is domiciled outside the UK is liable to inheritance tax in respect of their UK assets only.

The third statement is false because the current annual exemption must be used before any amount brought forward.

The final statement is false because the residence nil rate band is only available on a gift of a residence to a direct descendant on death, not during the donor's life.

(b)   (i)   Rowena makes a lifetime gift to a trust. The trust pays the inheritance tax on the gift at a rate of 20%.

(ii)   Ori gave £30,000 to his niece on 1 July 2013. In September 2021 Ori died. The gift of £30,000 will not be subject to inheritance tax on Ori's death.

   The gift was made more than seven years before Ori's death.

(iii)   Umar gave £2,600 to his brother on 1 July 2019. This was his only gift in the tax year 2019/20. Gary died on 1 December 2021. The gift of £2,600 will not be subject to inheritance tax.

   The annual exemption for the tax year 2019/20 covers the gift.

(c)

Gift	PET	CLT	Exempt
A painting worth £11,500 from Gomez to his civil partner.			✓
A sculpture worth £20,000 from James to his sister.	✓		

Tutorial note

The gift of the painting would be covered by the inter-spouse/civil partner exemption.

---

67   JOSHUA

(a)

	True	False
Taper relief reduces the inheritance tax on death on a gift made between three and seven years earlier.	✓	
Unused annual exemption can be transferred between spouses.		✓
A gift of £400 to a grandchild is reduced to £150 by the small gifts exemption.		✓
The rate of 40% applies for inheritance tax on death, whatever the level of the taxpayer's income.	✓	
The residence nil rate band is deducted from the inheritance tax charged on a residence left to a direct descendant on death.		✓

Tutorial note

The second statement is false because only unused nil rate band or residence nil rate band can be transferred, not the annual exemption.

The third statement is false because if the gift exceeds £250, the whole amount of the gift is chargeable (unless covered by other exemptions such as the annual exemption).

The final statement is false because the residence nil rate band reduces the amount of the death estate chargeable at 40%. It is not deducted from the tax charged.

(b)

(i)   Florence gave a house worth £430,000 to her son on 1 October 2015. Florence died on 1 May 2021.

The house .... be subject to inheritance tax in the UK following the death of Florence.

may	will not
✓	

(ii)   Jemima gave £370,000 to a trust on 1 September 2012. In June 2021 Jemima died.

Inheritance tax .... have been charged on the gift when it was made.

would	would not
✓	

(iii) Joshua is domiciled in France. He owns a house situated in the UK worth £675,000.

This house .... be subject to inheritance tax in the UK when Joshua dies.

will	will not
✓	

Tutorial note

(i)   *Florence's gift will be chargeable to inheritance tax because she died within seven years of making it. However, it could be covered by the nil rate band, if both Florence's nil rate band and that of a deceased spouse were available. There is not enough information in the question to confirm this. Florence's residence nil rate band will not be available to set against this gift, as it was not left in her death estate.*

(ii)   *A gift to a trust is a chargeable lifetime transfer. This gift exceeds the nil rate band and would have been subject to inheritance tax when it was made.*

(iii) *Joshua's house is situated in the UK and will be subject to UK inheritance tax regardless of where Joshua is domiciled.*

(c)

Gift	PET	CLT	Exempt
Cash of £10,000 given from father to daughter for her 21st birthday.	✓		
A sculpture worth £100,000 to the British Museum for national purposes.			✓

68   GAVIN

(a)

	True	False
A marriage exemption on a gift from a brother to his sister is £1,000.	✓	
A gift between two friends is not chargeable during the donor's lifetime.	✓	
Taper relief of 60% is available to reduce the lifetime tax on a chargeable lifetime transfer (CLT) made between five and six years before the donor's death.		✓
The annual exemption for a tax year is always wasted if there are no gifts made during that year.		✓
The residence nil rate band may be available if a death estate includes a residence which is left to a direct descendant.	✓	

Tutorial note

The third statement is false because taper relief reduces the death tax, not the lifetime tax.

The fourth statement is false because unused annual exemption can be carried forward one year.

(b) **(i)** Denise died in March 2022. She was a basic rate taxpayer for income tax purposes in the tax year 2021/22. Inheritance tax on her death estate is paid at a rate of 40%.

Tutorial note

The rate of inheritance tax on death is 40% and this does not depend on the taxpayer's level of income.

(ii) Frieda made a chargeable lifetime transfer on September 2015. The rate of taper relief available on this transfer on her death in February 2022 is 80%.

The CLT is made more than six years before death, but not more than seven years.

(iii) Jonathan made a gift of £4,000 to his son in January 2021 and a gift of £10,000 to his daughter in May 2021. These are Jonathan's only lifetime gifts. The amount of annual exemption set against the May 2021 gift is £3,000.

The gift to Jonathan's son uses the 2020/21 annual exemption of £3,000 in full, and £1,000 of the brought forward annual exemption from 2019/20. The unused amount of £2,000 from the tax year 2019/20 cannot be carried forward to the tax year 2021/22. The only available annual exemption in the tax year 2021/22 is that for the current year of £3,000.

(c)

Gift	PET	CLT	Exempt
Cash of £15,000 to a registered charity.			✓
Cash of £10,000 from a mother to her 12 year old son.	✓		

Tutorial note

Gifts between individuals who are not civil partners or spouses are potentially exempt transfers, regardless of age of the individuals.

69   MAISIE

(a)

	True	False
Taper relief applied to the inheritance tax due on a gift on death can lead to a repayment of tax.		✓
A gift to charity is exempt up to an amount of £3,000. The excess is chargeable.		✓
Unused nil rate band of a civil partner who has died can be transferred to the surviving partner for use on the death of the surviving partner.	✓	
The amount of the marriage exemption depends on the relationship between donor and donee.	✓	
A chargeable lifetime transfer made more than seven years before the donor's death is not chargeable to inheritance tax on death.	✓	

Tutorial note

The first statement is false because taper relief applies a percentage to reduce the death tax, and so can never give rise to a repayment.

The second statement is false because there is no limit on the exemption on a gift to charity.

(b)   (i)   Petra died on 31 December 2021. She had made no lifetime gifts during the tax years 2020/21 or 2021/22. The amount of annual exemption that can reduce Petra's chargeable death estate is £0.

Tutorial note

The annual exemption is only available for lifetime transfers. It cannot be used to reduce the death estate.

(ii)   Rob died in May 2021. His death estate included his home valued at £450,000. Rob had never married and left his estate to his brother on his death. The maximum amount of nil rate band and residence nil rate band that may be available on Rob's death is £325,000.

Tutorial note

The residence nil rate band is only available if the residence is left to a direct descendant.

(iii)   Inheritance tax paid on a particular chargeable lifetime transfer was charged at a rate of 20%. The tax was suffered by the donee on the occasion of the gift.

(c)

Gift	PET	CLT	Exempt
Gift of £50,000 between civil partners.			✓
Gift of £80,000 to a trust from an individual		✓	

Tutorial note

The first gift is covered by the civil partner exemption.

A gift to a trust is a chargeable lifetime transfer.

70 FRANCIS

(a)

	True	False
Gifts of cash of up to £250 between individuals are always exempt.		✓
A gift by any individual of £1,000 to someone getting married is exempt.	✓	
The annual exemption reduces the tax due on a chargeable lifetime transfer by £3,000.		✓
The residence nil rate band may be available if a grandmother leaves a residence to her grandson on death.	✓	
The annual exemption is applied to the first gift made in a tax year, even if this is a potentially exempt transfer.	✓	

Tutorial note

The first statement is false because the £250 limit applies per donee per tax year.

The third statement is false because the annual exemption reduces the amount of the transfer, not the tax.

(b) (i) Priti gave £7,000 to her daughter Siri on the occasion of Siri's marriage in January 2022. Priti has not made any other lifetime gifts. The amount of annual exemption that reduces the value of this gift is £2,000.

Tutorial note

The marriage exemption of £5,000 is deducted first, leaving only £2,000 to be covered by the annual exemption.

(ii) Garth died in November 2021. His wife had died in 2018 and had left her entire estate to Garth. Neither Garth nor his wife made any lifetime transfers. The maximum amount of nil rate band and residence nil rate band that may be available on Garth's death is £1,000,000.

Tutorial note

The gift to Garth on his wife's death was exempt and so used none of her nil rate band nor residence nil rate band. These are both available to Garth, as well as his own nil rate band and residence nil rate band i.e. 2 × £325,000 + 2 × £175,000 = £1,000,000.

(c)

Gift	PET	CLT	Exempt
Gift of £50,000 to a political party			✓
Gift of a car worth £12,000 to a friend	✓		
Gift of assets worth £60,000 to a trust		✓	

Tutorial note

A car is an exempt asset for capital gains tax but not for inheritance tax.

Section 3

MOCK ASSESSMENT QUESTIONS

ASSESSMENT INFORMATION

This assessment has 10 tasks.

You should therefore attempt and aim to complete EVERY task.

The total number of marks available for this assessment is 100.

Each task is independent. You will not need to refer to your answers to previous tasks.

Read every task carefully to make sure you understand what is required.

Where the date is relevant, it is given in the task data.

Both minus signs and brackets can be used to indicate negative numbers unless task instructions state otherwise.

You must use a full stop to indicate a decimal point. For example, write 100.57 NOT 100,57 or 10057.

You may use a comma to indicate a number in the thousands but you don't have to. For example, both 10000 and 10,000 are acceptable.

TASK 1 (10 marks)

This task is about the principles and rules underpinning tax.

(a) **Taxes can be referred to as progressive, regressive or proportional. Explain what is meant by each of these terms. Give an example of a progressive tax.** **(4 marks)**

Jadon was born in the UK. His parents both have UK domicile. He goes to work in Spain on 1 February 2022.

(b) (i) **Explain Jadon's residence and domicile for the tax year 2021/22.**

(ii) **Explain the effect Jadon's residence and domicile will have on his chargeability to UK tax.** **(6 marks)**

TASK 2 (14 marks)

This task is about income from employment.

Mandeep was unemployed until 6 June 2021, when he started a new job as a salesman.

As part of his remuneration package, he was provided with a company car. All necessary information regarding the car is detailed below.

Car	Mandeep
Number of months available	8 months
Car registration date	30 September 2020
Fuel details	Diesel
CO_2 emissions	137g/km
Cost price	£19,000
List price	£21,550
Employee contribution to the cost of the car	£2,500
Employee contribution to the use of the car	£20 per month
Private fuel provided by the employer	Yes
Employee contribution for part of the cost of the private fuel	£10 per month

(a) Complete the following table to show Mandeep's taxable benefits in kind for the car for the tax year 2021/22. Show monetary answers in whole pounds only.

(6 marks)

	Scale charge %	Amount £
Scale charge percentage		
Taxable benefit on provision of the car		
Taxable benefit on provision of the fuel		

Alice had the sole use of a company van for the whole of the tax year 2021/22. The van has CO_2 emissions of 129g/km and cost her employer £11,000. There is 50% private use of the van by Alice.

(b) Complete the following table to show Alice's taxable benefits in kind for the van for the tax year 2021/22. Enter your answer in whole pounds only. If your answer is zero, enter '0'.

(3 marks)

	Amount £
Taxable benefit on provision of the van	
Taxable benefit on provision of the fuel	

(c) Enter the amount that would be taxable for the tax year 2021/22 for each benefit in the box provided. Enter the amount in whole pounds only. If the amount is zero, enter '0'. Where appropriate use the averaging method.

(5 marks)

(i)	Carol's employer paid £6,700 to cover the costs she incurred when she relocated from Newcastle to Hull in order to start work in her new job.	£
(ii)	Bill received £1,800 as a loan from his employer throughout the tax year 2021/22. He pays interest on the loan at the rate of 1%.	£
(iii)	Les borrowed a digital camera from his employer on 6 June 2021 until 5 April 2022 to use on his holidays and for family occasions. The market value of the camera on 6 June 2021 was £1,200.	£
(iv)	From 6 January 2022, Farah was provided with a company loan of £22,000 on which she pays interest at 0.75% per annum.	£

TASK 3 (10 marks)

This task is about income from investments and property.

(a) **Complete the following sentences. Enter your answer in whole pounds only. If your answer is zero, enter '0'.** **(4 marks)**

    (i)   Simone received a dividend of £10,000. Her other taxable income, after personal allowances, total £145,000. The total tax payable by Simone on these dividends is:

        £

    (ii)   Noah received £1,800 in interest from his bank account and £80 in interest from a national savings certificate. His other taxable income, after personal allowances, total £25,000.

        Noah's income from investments on which tax will be paid is:

        £

        The total tax payable by Noah on the interest is:

        £

Sydney owns and rents out two properties in the tax year 2021/22. Relevant information on the properties is shown in the table below.

(b) **Complete the following table to show taxable rent and allowable expenses for these properties in the tax year 2021/22. Enter your answer in whole pounds only. If your answer is zero, enter '0'.** **(4 marks)**

Property	Details	Taxable rent £	Taxable expenses £
Astral way	Astral way was let until 28 February 2022 for rent of £800 a month payable on the 1st of the month. The property then remained empty until 1 July 2022. Sydney paid cleaning costs of £40 a month on the 30th of each month, and paid £80 to advertise for a new tenant on 1 April 2022.		
Albion Court	Albion Court was let from 1 June 2021 and was empty before this date (the previous tenant left in February 2021). On this date the tenant paid £14,000 of rent for the year to 31 May 2022. Sydney spent £1,200 on insurance on 1 July 2022 for the year ended 31 August 2022.		

(c) **Identify whether the following statements are true or false.** **(2 marks)**

	True	False
Landlords can claim a £1,000 property allowance as well as any actual expenses paid during the year		
A loss on property income can be offset against other income the taxpayer has in the year		

TASK 4 (14 marks)

This task is about income tax payable.

Rita is employed as a receptionist with a gross annual salary of £33,030. On 21 April 2021, she received a bonus of £4,435 which related to her performance during the year ended 31 March 2021. She has paid £4,993 of PAYE during the year.

Rita received dividends of £23,025 and ISA interest of £6,980.

During the tax year 2021/22 Rita paid 5% of her salary into an occupational pension scheme. Her employer paid 8% of her salary into the same scheme. Rita also gave £640 to charities through the gift aid scheme during the year.

Enter your answer and workings into the table below to calculate Rita's net income tax liability for the tax year 2021/22. Show the answer in whole pounds. **(12 marks)**

TASK 5 (6 marks)

This task is about national insurance contributions.

Laura is 41 years old and is employed by Plyo Ltd. In the tax year 2021/22 Laura received the following from her employer:

	£
Salary	73,000
Workplace childcare costing Plyo Ltd	2,800
Benefit in respect of company car	7,700

Laura incurred expenses of £5,120 wholly, exclusively and necessarily in the performance of her duties.

Plyo Ltd also employs Dustin on a part-time basis, paying him a salary of £19,500. Plyo Ltd is a large company employing a number of employees besides Laura and Dustin.

(a) **Complete the following sentences. Enter your answer in whole pounds only. If your answer is zero, enter '0'.**

    (i)   The total class 1 National Insurance contributions payable by Laura in the tax year 2021/22 are   (2 marks)

    (ii)   The class 1 employer National Insurance contributions payable by Plyo Ltd in respect of Laura in the tax year 2021/22 are   (1 mark)

    (iii)   The class 1A employer National Insurance contributions payable by Plyo Ltd in respect of Laura in the tax year 2021/22 are   (1 mark)

    (iv)   The total class 1 National Insurance contributions payable by Dustin in the tax year 2021/22 are   (1 mark)

(b) **Identify whether the following statement about National Insurance contributions is true or false.**   **(2 marks)**

	True	False
If the employer pays a mileage allowance in excess of the approved rates this excess is subject to class 1A NICs.		

TASK 6 (8 marks)

This task is about tax planning.

During the tax year 2021/22 Carissa received:

	£
Employment income	62,400
Interest from a bank account	2,240
Dividends from shares	1,250

(a) **Identify the effect on Carissa's income tax liability for the tax year 2021/22 if she had made each of the following changes. Assume that each of the changes is the only change made to the details above.** **(4 marks)**

Change	Increase	Decrease	No impact
Carissa sells the shares which generate her dividends.			
Carissa joins the company occupational pension scheme. She contributes 5% of her salary each month.			
Carissa's employer starts paying her business mileage at 45p a mile. Carissa will travel 6,000 business miles in the tax year.			
Carissa transfers a quarter of her savings from her bank account to an ISA. The amount of interest earned from both accounts would remain the same as she is currently earning.			

Today's date is 1 April 2021.

Niamh is a higher rate taxpayer, and also earns £500 of savings income a year.

She has just inherited £300,000 from her uncle, and is considering how to invest the funds. She does not wish to invest in shares, as she considers this risky. Instead, she is considering investing the money in a bank deposit account, which will earn approximately £9,000 of interest during the tax year 2021/22 at an average rate of 3%.

Alternatively, Niamh may consider investing in other types of bank account and/or transferring some or all of her inheritance to her husband Roberto for him to invest instead.

You should assume that any investments made will earn 3% interest per annum.

Roberto has taxable income of £30,700, which is all employment income.

(b) **Complete the following sentences. Enter your answers in whole pounds only. If your answer is zero, enter '0'.** **(4 marks)**

(i) How much tax will the couple save if both Niamh and Roberto invest the maximum amount each in an ISA rather than a standard bank account?

[   ]

(ii) How much tax will the couple save by if Niamh transfers sufficient funds to Roberto to utilise his savings allowance for the tax year 2021/22?

[   ]

(iii) To the nearest pound, how much tax will the couple save if in addition to point (ii) above the rest of the funds are transferred to Roberto before investment in the bank deposit account?

[   ]

TASK 7 (10 marks)

This task is about capital gains tax principles.

(a) **Identify whether the following sentences are true or false.** (3 marks)

	True	False
If an asset is transferred to a taxpayer's spouse the transfer is deemed to take place at market value for capital gains tax purposes.		
A gift of an asset to a charity is an exempt disposal for capital gains tax purposes		
A sale of a car is a chargeable disposal for capital gains tax purposes.		

Paul made a number of disposals of capital assets during the tax year 2021/22. The disposals have been made to unconnected persons.

(b) **Calculate the amount chargeable to capital gains tax (CGT) in the tax year 2021/22 for each asset disposed of below. If your answer is zero, enter '0'. Enter your answer in whole pounds only.** (7 marks)

Asset	Details	Chargeable to CGT £
Land	Paul inherited seven acres of land in August 2016 from his grandfather. The land had cost his grandfather £15,000 but was worth £49,000 (the probate value) when Paul received it. Paul sold three acres in November 2021 for £75,000 when the remaining four acres were worth £125,000. He paid auctioneer's commission of 8% when he sold the land.	
Racehorse	Paul sold a racehorse for £25,000. He had originally purchased the racehorse for £8,900.	
Holiday cottage	Paul sold a holiday cottage in Devon for £110,000. He originally purchased the cottage for £50,000 and extended it two years later which cost £8,000.	
Table	Paul sold an antique table to his neighbour for £5,000. He paid £50 commission on the sale. He originally purchased the table for £11,000. The table got scratched while he owned it (hence the low proceeds).	

TASK 8 (8 marks)

This task is about capital gains tax: disposals of shares.

Armand holds shares in Sun Ltd and has made a number of transactions over the years. Details of the transactions are:

		Number of shares	Cost/Proceeds
October 2015	Purchase	1,000	£1,250
January 2016	Purchase	3,000	£6,300
December 2017	Bonus issue	1 for 3	
January 2018	Purchase	5,000	£15,200
October 2021	Sale	9,000	£5 a share

Clearly showing the balance of shares, and their value to carry forward, calculate the gain or loss made on these shares.

All workings must be shown in your calculations. **(8 marks)**

TASK 9 (10 marks)

This task is about capital gains tax: reliefs and exemptions.

(a) **Identify whether the following statements about capital gains tax are true or false.**

(4 marks)

	True	False
If a taxpayer has adjusted total income greater than £100,000 in the year the annual exempt amount will be restricted.		
A higher rate taxpayer will pay CGT at 20%.		
Capital losses that cannot be used in the current year are carried back.		
Any unused annual exempt amount can be carried forward one year.		

Hamza bought a house for £101,000 on 1 March 1999.

He lived in the house with his wife until 31 March 2003 when they went to work in Newcastle.

He returned to the house on 1 April 2013 and lived in it until 31 July 2020 when he moved in with his elderly parents.

The house was sold for £336,000 on 30 April 2021.

(b) **Complete the following sentence. Enter your answer in whole pounds only. If your answer is zero, enter '0'.** **(2 marks)**

The total amount that Hamza will pay capital gains tax on, after all allowances, is

Magda has disposed of several capital assets in the tax year 2021/22 and realised the following gains and losses:

	Disposal to:	£
Chargeable gain	Aunt	23,000
Chargeable gain	Unconnected person	14,800
Allowable loss	Brother	(3,000)
Allowable loss	Friend	(2,600)

In the tax year 2020/21 Magda had capital gains of £20,000 and capital losses of £25,600.

The AEA for the tax year 2020/21 is £12,300.

(c) **Complete the following sentences. Enter your answer in whole pounds only. If your answer is zero, enter '0'.** **(3 marks)**

    (i)   The amount chargeable, if any, to capital gains tax for the tax year 2021/22 is

£ _____

    (ii)   The amount of losses, if any, to carry forward to the tax year 2022/23 is

£ _____

Charbel has taxable income of £35,700 for the tax year 2020/21. He has made gains of £26,800 on the sale of shares.

(d) **Complete the following sentence. Enter your answer in whole pounds only. If your answer is zero, enter '0'.** **(1 marks)**

The total of Charbel's capital gains tax payable in the tax year 2021/22 is £ _____

TASK 10 (10 MARKS)

This task is about inheritance tax.

(a)   Identify whether the following statements about inheritance tax (IHT) are true or false.

(5 marks)

	True	False
A transfer to a discretionary trust will be subject to IHT when the transfer is made.		
A gift to a spouse or civil partner is only exempt if that gift is made in the death estate.		
Sunisa leaves her house in her estate to her son. The residence nil rate band will be available when calculating the death tax due.		
Lifetime tax is paid at 20% on the excess over the nil rate band, unless the donor pays the tax.		
The available nil rate band is reduced by gross chargeable transfers made in the five years before this transfer.		

(b)   Complete the following statements that relate to inheritance tax (IHT).

(2 marks)

The small gifts exemption is available if a gift does not exceed [£100/£250/£500/£3000].

Kenny made a chargeable lifetime transfer in June 2018. He died in September 2021. Taper relief will be available at [0%/20%/40%] when calculating death tax.

Laura lives in the UK and has only made three gifts during her lifetime.

(c)   Complete the table below to show whether these gifts would be an exempt transfer (ET) or potentially exempt transfer (PET).   (3 marks)

	Details of the gift	Value £	ET or PET
13 September 2014	Gift to her granddaughter on her 21st birthday	30,000	
24 December 2020	Gift to the RSPCA (national charity)	10,000	
14 February 2021	Gift to her son on his wedding	70,000	

Section 4

MOCK ASSESSMENT ANSWERS

TASK 1

(a) A proportional tax is one that takes the same proportion of income as income rises.

A regressive tax is one whereby the proportion of income taken as tax reduces as income rises.

Under a progressive tax the proportion of income that tax represents increases as the person's income increases.

Income tax is a progressive tax. The rate of tax charged rises as the level of income increases.

(b) Jadon is UK domiciled. He has a UK domicile of origin taking the domicile of his father.

He is also UK resident in the tax year 2021/22. He is automatically classed as UK resident as he was in the UK in the tax year for more than 183 days.

As he is UK resident and domiciled he will pay income tax in the UK on his worldwide income.

TASK 2

(a)

	Scale charge %	Amount £
Scale charge percentage	35	
Taxable benefit on provision of the car		4,285
Taxable benefit on provision of the fuel		5,740

Workings

(W1) Appropriate percentage

CO_2 emissions are rounded down to 135g/km.

Appropriate percentage = (15% + 4% diesel + (135 − 55) × 1/5) = 35%

(W2) Car taxable benefit

Car has been available for 8 months of the tax year.

	£
(£21,550 − £2,500) × 35% × 8/12	4,445
Less: Contribution in respect of private use (£20 × 8 months)	(160)
Car benefit	4,285

Tutorial note

The car has CO_2 emissions in excess of 55g/km.

The appropriate percentage is therefore calculated in the normal way (i.e. 15% for petrol cars plus 4% for diesel cars, plus 1% for each complete 5g/km above 55g/km up to a maximum percentage of 37%).

As the car has not been available all year, the benefit must be time apportioned.

Contributions towards the cost of the car are an allowable deduction from the list price (up to a maximum of £5,000) before multiplying by the relevant percentage.

Contributions in respect of the private use of the car are an allowable deduction from the benefit.

(W3) Fuel benefit

Fuel benefit = (£24,600 × 35% × 8/12) = £5,740

Tutorial note

The appropriate percentage for the fuel benefit is the same as that calculated for the car benefit. This is applied to a fixed scale figure of £24,600.

As the fuel was not provided all year, the benefit must be time apportioned.

A contribution towards the provision of private fuel is not an allowable deduction from the benefit.

(b)

	Amount £
Taxable benefit on provision of the van	3,500
Taxable benefit on provision of the fuel	669

Tutorial note

If the employee is provided with private use of a van (unless private use is insignificant) the benefit is £3,500 per annum. Private fuel provided for the van gives an additional benefit of £669 per annum.

Both these figures can be found in your tax tables.

(i)	Carol's employer paid £6,700 to cover the costs she incurred when she relocated from Newcastle to Hull in order to start work in her new job.	£0	W1
(ii)	Bill received £1,800 as a loan from his employer throughout 2021/22. He pays interest on the loan at the rate of 1%.	£0	W2
(iii)	Les borrowed a digital camera from his employer on 6 June 2021 until 5 April 2022 to use on his holidays and for family occasions. The market value of the camera on 6 June 2021 was £1,200.	£200	W3
(iv)	From 6 January 2022, Farah was provided with a company loan of £22,000 on which she pays interest at 0.75% per annum.	£69	W4

Workings

(W1) Relocation costs

Taxable benefit = £0

Tutorial note

Removal expenses of up to £8,000 are exempt when incurred in relation to a new employment or if an employee's job is relocated.

(W2) Company loan

Taxable benefit = £0

Tutorial note

Loans that do not exceed £10,000 at any time in the tax year are an exempt benefit.

(W3) Use of camera

Taxable benefit = (£1,200 × 20% × 10/12) = £200

Tutorial note

The benefit for the use of a company asset such as a camera is 20% of the market value of the asset when first made available to the employee.

As the camera was only made available to Les from 6 June 2021, the benefit is time apportioned.

(W4) Company loan

Taxable benefit = (£22,000 × (2.00% – 0.75%) × 3/12) = £69

Tutorial note

Beneficial loan interest benefit is calculated as follows:

= Outstanding loan × the difference between the official rate of interest (2% in the tax year 2021/22) and the actual interest rate paid by the employee.

However, as the loan was provided nine months into the tax year 2021/22, the benefit must be time apportioned, as the rates of interest quoted are annual rates of interest.

TASK 3

(a)   (i)   The answer is £2,880.

(ii)   The answers are £800 and £160.

(W1) Tax on dividends

Simone's remaining higher rate band = £150,000 – £145,000 = £5,000

Tax on her dividends is calculated as:

(£2,000 × 0%) + (£3,000 × 32.5%) + (£5,000 × 38.1%) = £2,880

Tutorial note

The tax on dividends uses what is left of Simone's bands for income tax after other income. Her basic rate band has been fully utilised by other income.

Simone is entitled to a dividend allowance of £2,000. This uses up some of the remaining £5,000 of the higher rate band so only £3,000 remains.

(W2) Tax on interest

Tax on Noah's interest is calculated as:

(£1,000 × 0%) + (£800 × 20%) = £160

Tutorial note

Noah's interest from a national savings certificate is exempt from tax.

He must pay tax on the bank interest. He has £12,700 (£37,700 – £25,000) of his basic rate band left so all this income will fall within the basic rate band.

As a basic rate taxpayer he is entitled to a personal savings allowance of £1,000. The rest of his savings income is subject to income tax at 20%.

(b)

Property	Details	Taxable rent £	Taxable expenses £
Astral way	Astral way was let until 28 February 2022 for rent of £800 a month payable on the 1st of the month. The property then remained empty until 1 July 2022. Sydney paid cleaning costs of £40 a month on the 30th of each month, and paid £80 to advertise for a new tenant on 1 April 2022.	8,000	560
Albion Court	Albion Court was let from 1 June 2021 and was empty before this date (the previous tenant left in February 2021). On this date the tenant paid £14,000 of rent for the year to 31 May 2022. Sydney spent £1,200 on insurance on 1 July 2021 for the year ended 31 August 2022.	14,000	1,200

(W1) Taxable rent – Astral way

Sydney is taxed on the rent received between 6 April 2021 and 5 April 2022.

10 × £800 = £8,000

(W2) Taxable expenses – Astral way

Expenses paid between 6 April 2021 and 5 April 2022.

(12 × £40) + £80 = £560

Tutorial note

As Sydney's gross rents do not exceed £150,000 her rent will be assessed under the cash basis unless she makes an election for the accruals basis to apply.

Under the cash basis rent is assessable when it is received, and expenses are deductible in the period they are paid.

(c)

	True	False
Landlords can claim a £1,000 property allowance as well as any actual expenses paid during the year		✓
A loss on property income can be offset against other income the taxpayer has in the year		✓

Tutorial note

The property allowance can be claimed instead of actual property expenses, not as well as these.

Property losses can be offset against property income only. If these cannot be offset against other property profits in the year they are carried forward and offset against future property income.

TASK 4

Rita – Income tax computation – 2021/22

	Non-savings £	Dividends £	Total £
Salary	33,030		
Bonus (received 21 April 2021)	4,435		
Less: Employee's pension contribution (5% × £33,030)	(1,652)		
Employment income	35,813		35,813
Dividends		23,025	23,025
ISA interest – exempt			0
Net income	35,813	23,025	58,838
Less: PA	(12,570)		(12,570)
Taxable income	23,243	23,025	46,268

Income tax:

Non-savings income – basic rate	23,243 × 20%	4,649
Dividend income – dividend allowance	2,000 × 0%	0
Dividend income – basic rate	13,257 × 7.5%	994
	38,500	
Dividend income	7,768 × 32.5%	2,525
	46,268	
Income tax liability		8,168
Less: PAYE		(4,993)
Net income tax liability/Income tax payable		3,175

Working – BRB: £37,700 + ((100/80) × £640) = £38,500

Key answer tips

It is important when using this type of layout to analyse the taxable income into 'non-savings income', 'savings' and 'dividends' as different rates of tax apply to the different sources of income.

Note that:

- the above layout should be possible if the CBA gives five columns to complete the calculation

- the total lines cannot be inserted in the real CBA

- you may find it useful to do the computation on paper first before inputting on screen.

You may only be provided with three columns in the CBA. If this is the case, you may find it useful to write your answer up on paper first using all five columns, then type the total column only into the pro forma.

The employee pension contribution is an allowable deduction from employment income. The employer's contribution is exempt and has no input on the tax computation.

The basic rate band is extended by the gross gift aid donation.

TASK 5

(a) (i) The answer is £5,339.

Working

	£
(£50,270 – £9,568) × 12%	4,884
(£73,000 – £50,270) × 2%	455
	5,339

(ii) The answer is £8,854.

Working

(£73,000 – £8,840) × 13.8%	£8,854

(iii) The answer is £1,063.

Working

	£
Benefit in respect of company car	7,700
Workplace childcare	0
	7,700
£7,700 × 13.8%	1,063

(iv)   The answer is £1,192.

Working

(£19,500 – £9,568) × 12%   £1,192

Tutorial note

No deduction is available for expenses incurred wholly, exclusively and necessarily in the performance of duties when calculating earnings for the purposes of national insurance contributions.

The workplace childcare is an exempt benefit, such that it is not subject to class 1A contributions.

(b)

	True	False
If the employer pays a mileage allowance in excess of the approved rates this excess is subject to class 1A NICs.		✓

Tutorial note

Payments of mileage in excess of a flat 45p/mile are subject to class 1 NICs, not class 1A.

TASK 6

(a)

Change	Increase	Decrease	No impact
Carissa sells the shares which generate her dividends.			✓
Carissa joins the company occupational pension scheme. She contributes 5% of her salary each month.		✓	
Carissa's employer starts paying her business mileage at 45p a mile. Carissa will travel 6,000 business miles in the tax year.			✓
Carissa transfers a quarter of her savings from her bank account to an ISA. The amount of interest earned from both accounts would remain the same as she is currently earning.		✓	

Tutorial note

Carissa's dividends would not be subject to tax as they are covered by the dividend allowance.

An employee's contribution to an occupational pension scheme is an allowable deduction from employment income so will decrease her taxable income, in turn decreasing her tax liability.

The mileage amount paid is equal to the HMRC approved amounts. This will have no impact on Carissa's tax.

Transferring savings to an ISA will generate exempt income. Her bank account interest in excess of her personal savings allowance (£500 as a higher rate taxpayer) is subject to tax.

(b) (i) £360

Both Niamh and Roberto can invest £20,000 into an ISA in the tax year 2021/22. The interest earned will then be exempt from income tax, and will therefore save Niamh tax on that interest at 40% and Roberto tax on the interest at 20%. The tax saving will be £360 (£20,000 × 3% × 40%) + (£20,000 × 3% × 20%).

(ii) £400

Roberto is a basic rate taxpayer, and therefore has an unused savings allowance of £1,000. By transferring enough of her investment to Roberto to utilise this allowance, Niamh will save tax of £400 (£1,000 × 40%).

(iii) £1,200

Roberto has taxable income of £30,700, so he has an unused basic rate band of £7,000 (£37,700 – £30,700). £1,000 of this basic rate band will be utilised by the £1,000 covered by his savings allowance (see above) so he has a further £6,000 of basic rate band available. Any savings income falling in this band will be taxed at 20% for Roberto, rather than 40% for Niamh. By transferring a further amount of her investment to Roberto to utilise this band, Niamh will save tax of £1,200 (£6,000 × (40% – 20%)).

Tutorial note

Niamh's own savings allowance of £500 will be used by her existing savings income.

TASK 7

(a)

	True	False
If an asset is transferred to a taxpayer's spouse the transfer is deemed to take place at market value for capital gains tax purposes.		✓
A gift of an asset to a charity is an exempt disposal for capital gains tax purposes	✓	
A sale of a car is a chargeable disposal for capital gains tax purposes.		✓

Tutorial note

A transfer between spouses is deemed to take place on a no gain no loss basis.

A car is an exempt asset for capital gains tax purposes.

(b)

Asset	Details	Chargeable to CGT £
Land	Paul inherited seven acres of land in August 2016 from his grandfather. The land had cost his grandfather £15,000 but was worth £49,000 (the probate value) when Paul received it. Paul sold three acres in November 2021 for £75,000 when the remaining four acres were worth £125,000. He paid auctioneer's commission of 8% when he sold the land.	50,625
Racehorse	Paul sold a racehorse for £25,000. He had originally purchased the racehorse for £8,900.	0
Holiday cottage	Paul sold a holiday cottage in Devon for £110,000. He originally purchased the cottage for £50,000 and extended it two years later which cost £8,000.	52,000
Table	Paul sold an antique table to his neighbour for £5,000. He paid £50 commission on the sale. He originally purchased the table for £11,000. The table got scratched while he owned it (hence the low proceeds).	(5,050)

Workings

(W1) Antique table

The answer is £50,625.

	£
Proceeds	75,000
Less: Auction fees (£75,000 × 8%)	(6,000)
	———
	69,000
Less: Cost £49,000 × (£75,000/(£75,000 + £125,000))	(18,375)
	———
Chargeable gain	50,625
	———

Tutorial note

If a taxpayer inherits an asset, its cost when calculating the chargeable gain on its disposal is its value at death; also referred to as the probate value.

Note that this rule is similar to receiving a gift where the cost is the market value at the date of receipt.

With a part disposal of the land, the cost must be apportioned using the A/A+B formula NOT on the proportion of acreage sold.

Note that A is the gross sale proceeds, before deducting the auctioneers' fees.

A racehorse is a wasting chattel and is exempt from capital gains tax.

(W2) Holiday cottage

	£
Proceeds	110,000
Less: Cost	(50,000)
Extension	(8,000)
	———
Chargeable gain	52,000
	———

(W3) Antique table

	£
Deemed proceeds	6,000
Less: Selling costs	(50)
	———
	5,950
Less: Cost	(11,000)
	———
Allowable loss	(5,050)
	———

Tutorial note

An antique table is a non-wasting chattel and as it cost > £6,000 and proceeds are < £6,000, special rules apply.

The gross proceeds are deemed to be £6,000 in the allowable loss calculation.

TASK 8

Chargeable gain calculation

	£
Proceeds (9,000 × £5)	45,000
Less: Cost (W)	(19,815)
	———
Chargeable gain	25,185
	———

Working: Share pool

		Number	Cost £
Oct 2015	Purchase	1,000	1,250
Jan 2016	Purchase	3,000	6,300
		———	———
		4,000	7,550
Dec 2017	Bonus issue (1 for 3)	1,333	Nil
Jan 2018	Purchase	5,000	15,200
		———	———
		10,333	22,750
Oct 2021	Sale (£22,750 × 9,000/10,333)	(9,000)	(19,815)
		———	———
Balance c/f		1,333	2,935
		———	———

TASK 9

(a)

	True	False
If a taxpayer has adjusted total income greater than £100,000 in the year the annual exempt amount will be restricted.		✓
A higher rate taxpayer will pay CGT at 20%.	✓	
Capital losses that cannot be used in the current year are carried back.		✓
Any unused annual exempt amount can be carried forward one year.		✓

Tutorial note

The annual exempt amount is available in full to all taxpayers. Their level of income has no effect on this.

Capital losses that cannot be used in the current year can be carried forward only.

The annual exempt amount can only be used in the year it relates to. Any unused amounts are lost.

(b) The answer is £19,805.

	£
Sale proceeds	336,000
Less: Cost	(101,000)
	———
	235,000
Less: PRR (£235,000 × 230/266) (W)	(203,195)
	———
Chargeable gain	31,805
Less: AEA	(12,300)
	———
Taxable gain	19,505
	———

Working: PPR relief

	Total months	Exempt months	Chargeable months
1 Mar 1999 — 31 Mar 2003 Owner occupied	49	49	
1 Apr 2003 — 31 Mar 2013 Working in Newcastle	120	84 (Note 1)	36
1 Apr 2013 — 31 Jul 2020 Owner occupied	88	88	
1 Aug 2020 — 30 April 2021 Empty	9	9 (Note 2)	
	266	230	36

Tutorial note

1   *Of the 120 months working in Newcastle, a maximum of 48 months are deemed occupation as 'working elsewhere in the UK' and a further 36 months are then allowed as deemed occupation for any reason.*

As these periods are both preceded and followed by periods of actual occupation they qualify as deemed periods of occupation.

Total period of deemed occupation is therefore 84 months (48 + 36).

2   *The last nine months of ownership is always allowed.*

Remember to deduct the annual exempt amount!

(c)   **(i)**   **Taxable gain**

	£
Chargeable gains (£23,000 + £14,800)	37,800
Less: Current year allowable losses (Note)	(2,600)
	35,200
Less: Annual exempt amount	(12,300)
	22,900
Less: Capital losses brought forward (£25,600 – £20,000) (Note)	(5,600)
Taxable gain	17,300

   (ii)   **Capital loss left to carry forward**

Loss on disposal to brother (Note)	3,000

Tutorial note

The loss arising on the disposal to the brother is a connected person loss. It cannot be set against other gains. It can only be carried forward and set against gains arising from disposals to the same brother in the future.

The capital losses made in the tax year 2020/21 are automatically set off as far as possible against the gains in the same tax year. This means £20,000 of the losses are utilised in the tax year 2020/21 and the AEA is wasted. The remaining capital losses of £5,600 are carried forward and offset against future net gains after the deduction of the AEA.

(d)   **(i)**   **Capital gains tax liability**

	£
Capital gains	26,800
Less: Annual exempt amount	(12,300)
Taxable gains	14,500

£		
2,000 (W)	× 10%	200
12,500	× 20%	2,500
14,500		2,700

Working

	£
Basic rate band	37,700
Less: Taxable income	(35,700)
Basic rate band unused	2,000

Tutorial note

Chargeable gains are taxed at 10% if they fall below the basic rate threshold and 20% if they fall above the threshold.

TASK 10

(a)

	True	False
A transfer to a discretionary trust will be subject to IHT when the transfer is made.	✓	
A gift to a spouse or civil partner is only exempt if that gift is made in the death estate.		✓
Sunisa leaves her home in her estate to her son. The residence nil rate band will be available when calculating the death tax due.	✓	
Lifetime tax is paid at 20% on the excess over the nil rate band, unless the donor pays the tax.	✓	
The available nil rate band is reduced by gross chargeable transfers made in the five years before this transfer.		✓

Tutorial note

Chargeable lifetime transfers (CLT) are subject to tax when the gift is made with a further charge being made if the donor dies within seven years of the gift.

Gifts to spouses are exempt if the gift is made during lifetime or in the death estate.

The residence nil rate band is available when a residence is left on death to a direct descendant.

*The nil rate band is reduced by gross chargeable transfers in the **seven** years before this one*

(b) The small gifts exemption is available if a gift does not exceed **£250**.

Kenny made a chargeable lifetime transfer in June 2018. He died in September 2021. Taper relief will be available at **20%** when calculating death tax.

Tutorial note

Taper relief is available to reduce death tax on lifetime gifts once the donor has survived more than three years from making the gift. Kenny survived three whole years so the relevant percentage reduction is 20%.

(c)

	Details of the gift	Value £	ET or PET
13 September 2014	Gift to her granddaughter on her 21st birthday	30,000	PET
24 December 2020	Gift to the RSPCA (national charity)	10,000	ET
14 February 2021	Gift to her son on his wedding	70,000	PET